THE CITY SLICKER'S HANDBOOK

Peter Pugh

Cartoons by

Michael Heath and Peattie & Taylor

MICHAEL JOSEPH
LONDON

MICHAEL JOSEPH LTD

Published by the Penguin Group
27 Wrights Lane, London W8 5TZ, England
Viking Penguin Inc, 40 West 23rd Street, New York,
New York 10010, USA
Penguin Books Australia Ltd, Ringwood, Victoria, Australia
Penguin Books Canada Ltd, 2801 John Street, Markham, Ontario,
Canada L3R 1B4
Penguin Books (NZ) Ltd, 182-190 Wairau Road, Auckland 10, New
Zealand

Penguin Books Ltd, Registered Offices: Harmondsworth, Middlesex,
England

First published 1988

Designed and produced by Genesis Productions Limited
30 Great Portland Street, London W1N 5AD

Copyright © Genesis Productions Limited 1988

Main text: Peter Pugh
Additional text: Gwyn Headley and Ian Irvine
Original cartoons: Michael Heath and Peattie & Taylor
Original photography: Brian Harris of *The Independent*
Designer: Jane Ewart
Editor: Rosemary Anderson

A CIP catalogue record for this book is available from the British Library.

ISBN 0-7181-3117-7

Printed and bound in Great Britain by
Butler & Tanner Ltd, Frome and London

CONTENTS

4

If the City were in the middle of the African jungle, David Attenborough would have gone there and we would have marvelled at the weird creatures that live in its crowded hothouse. But since it's in the middle of London we are only vaguely aware of its exotic species, highly specialized creatures superbly designed for survival in a strange and dangerous habitat: pure money. Sharks have to keep moving in order to breathe: so does the City. It is still the most important financial centre in the world, and has been for more than a century and a half, but it has only stayed that way by radical change. It may look much the same as it did 20 years ago – give or take a few show-off shiny buildings – and the crowds in the streets may seem the perennial men in suits, but don't be fooled. Behind the stiff fronts the offices have been transformed by high technology, and those people are doing jobs which didn't exist a few years ago, or if they did have been transformed out of recognition: new markets (commodities, Eurobonds, financial futures), new techniques (leveraged buy-outs, privatization, currency swops), new technology (computers, Big Bang).

Something happened in the the last 20 years: the world got richer and the world got smaller. More money than ever before moves round the world faster than ever before. The City was only too happy to oblige the nouveau riche nations like Saudi Arabia by advising them on investment. With this explosion in financial services, the City now thinks globally, and the carousel never stops, the markets never close. London – New York – Tokyo – London – New York – Tokyo .... And, of course, there's the money earned by the City's workforce. Gold, bonds, dollars, pounds, yen, deutschmarks, francs ... this industry's raw material passes through the City in billions every day and the rewards for its workers are correspondingly huge. The newspapers run stories about yuppy Porsches and property, but they're just the top dressing to an eighties' world which has given incomes in hundreds of thousands to people in their twenties. The disadvantage of this world is that it can fire you over the Tannoy, as many learnt after the Crash of '87.

New Improved City is a much slicker and sleeker place than the bowler-hat old-school version which remains in the popular imagination. It does well for Britain and it does well for itself. It's faster, harsher, more exciting and more fun than it used to be ... for some. Just like life in the UK.

Far left: Toiling termites in the Lloyd's compound
Left: Natives at LIFFE negotiating with their fingers

-1- THE THATCHER REVOLUTION

The British are a conservative people. That doesn't mean we are all Tories – but we do love stability, the status quo and tradition. We are incapable of organizing a car factory so that people turn up and leave on time, but give us a royal wedding and we will have everyone in their proper place hours beforehand. We cannot always have been so unadventurous; how else did we get our Empire? But we became stuck in our ways, perhaps to try and preserve what our forefathers had acquired and to protect it against parvenu foreigners.

Loss of power and influence

Unfortunately the rest of the world began to prefer what these other nations offered them, and Britain's global influence declined. It was slow at first, but was helped along by two world wars. Faced with this distressing loss of wealth, and therefore also of power and influence, and the slowly dawning realization that we, the nominal winners of those two wars, had somehow finished up as losers, we withdrew into our conservative shell even more. We wanted the good old days back, and maybe if we didn't allow any changes they would come back. Whether it was the politicians, whose major concern was scoring points off each other, or the middle classes who worried about preserving their station in society, or the trade unions who were intent on proving that industrial action was the greatest misnomer in the English language, the fact remained that the bright new Elizabethan Britain responded to the new and changing post-war world by burying its head in the sand and clinging to old, restrictive ways. For many years the reality was hidden because everyone's lot improved in absolute terms, even if in relation to the standard of living of our foreign rivals it declined at an alarming rate. Just as some people were

gloomily forecasting Armageddon, when Absolute Decline would set in, there arrived on the scene a new Boadicea, a new Queen Bess – Margaret Thatcher. In her view the British had reached the stage where they were like a lot of sulky little children keener on squabbling over who had the best place in the gutter than on getting up on the pavement and fighting with the best of them. Some people had already noticed her line with sulky children when, as Minister of Health, she took away their free milk allowance, earning herself the sobriquet Thatcher the Snatcher.

In truth Thatcher came to power in 1979 on her promise to bash the unions and knock them off the ridiculously high pedestal they had built for themselves. With the odd bloody battle along the way she certainly did that, although as Britain always has done in time of strife she had to call in old overseas allies, a South African and a Yankee Scot, to lead the troops in the two most difficult skirmishes. Michael Edwardes was the standard-bearer at British Leyland, and Ian MacGregor pinned her colours to his helmet at the National Coal Board. Having blown the cold wind of competition through one section of our business life – curbing the unions with sensible laws and a blast of unemployment, and management with a devastating exchange rate – she turned her beady eye on that other bastion of conservatism, the City.

THE NEW BOADICEA

Supernanny zaps the unions

The City of yesterday was important, make no mistake about it. However sorry we may have been feeling for ourselves in the last 30 years, we have been a great trading nation for hundreds of years and the City has been an integral part of that. No money, no ships. No ships, no trade.

But as the City grew and prospered on the back of trade, and vice versa, a nice little series of cartels grew up. Put two or three businessmen together and you have the basis of a cartel – let's stop undercutting each other, one of them suggests; if we all charge the same we can all get a slice of the cake without having to work for it. By the fifties and sixties these cartels were well established, and the City had nodded into somnolent complacency. A typical merchant banker arrived at his office every weekday morning at 9.30 prompt, dressed in his immaculate bespoke dark suit and a boiled white shirt with stiff collar. He was bowed in by deferential staff who took his umbrella and bowler hat from him, and was then brought his morning coffee and rich tea biscuits by a uniformed attendant. He would send for a head of department whom he would address as Mr Williams or, if he was feeling particularly pleased with life, as Williams. In return Williams would murmur, 'Yes, Mr Cecil, everything is running quite smoothly.'

And, indeed, everything was running smoothly – no nasty lurches in sterling, no sudden changes in interest rates, no violent upheavals in equities, no panics on Wall Street, no aggressive bids by upstarts yet to appear. After establishing that all was properly serene, Mr Cecil would dictate a few letters to his secretary, Miss Plumtree, half of them to do with his social and extra-curricular activities, and then join his colleagues for sherry. Conversation might touch on business but probably only in a general sense, as in 'I've got that chap Chambers from ICI coming in next week. Wants to issue some shares at some stage. We can handle that for him, can't we?' They would then move off to lunch, which would be long, substantial and of indifferent quality. The wine, however, would be good, and the port excellent. At 3.30 it

Agreeable dealing before Big Bang: the Stock Exchange 1951

would be time to check the closing index – the FT Index was up 1.3 to 337.4 – sign those letters and think about catching the train home after a cup of tea in front of the open fire in his office. As he walked to Bank underground station, Cecil might think idly that it was about time some of those bomb sites were filled in, and how miraculous it was that so many Wren churches had been saved from the Blitz.

Covering the overheads

If this was the life at a merchant bank, his travelling companions who worked in the clearing banks or as jobbers or stockbrokers enjoyed an equally comfortable and untroubled existence. Stockbrokers in particular had managed to increase their rates of commission, and as they did not act as principals they were theoretically immune from risk, apart from not covering their overheads. As those overheads consisted mainly of their immense salaries and partnership fees, there was not a major problem. Believe it or not, in spite of the staggering remuneration now being paid in the City, since the 1950s salaries have actually declined as a proportion of fixed overheads.

Jobbers had to keep their wits about them a little more as they had to make large financial commitments in buying stock and holding it on their books. Sharp movements in prices either way could cause them heavy losses. If prices moved down sharply, the stock they were holding and had to pay for would clearly be worth less, and some of it might even be unsaleable. If prices moved up, theoretically the jobbers should be in clover because the stock they held would be increasing in value – but sometimes they would have sold stock they did not yet hold and would be forced to buy at a higher price.

Overall it was a relatively tranquil exist-

JOBBERS The dealers on the Stock Exchange floor before Big Bang through whom the stockbroker had to buy and sell shares. They had no direct contact with the public. Nowadays they are called **market-makers** (and just to complicate things some stockbrokers are also now called market-makers).

ence. The hours were short, the weekends long and the margins good, and there was just enough takeover action for everyone to make a modest killing every so often. No one talked about insider dealing. They simply dealt on the information they had been given.

London gets bypassed

It couldn't go on. Thatcher did not like it because it was inefficient and restrictive. By the beginning of the 1980s, with the world rapidly becoming smaller, many financial deals were bypassing London because of its costs and restrictions. Stockbrokers were driving business overseas. Thatcher had removed Exchange Controls as soon as she came to power in 1979, so why buy a million ICI shares in London, and pay thousands of pounds in commission, when you could buy them in New York and pay hundreds of dollars?

As in industry, so in the City. Redundant dockers, miners and steel workers had been bought out of their jobs with lump sums; now the partners in jobbing and broking firms were bought out of theirs as an agreement in 1982 made it possible for large financial institutions, both British and overseas, to increase their stake in them from 10 to 29.9%. From March 1986 they were allowed 100% control.

A redundant long-serving miner might get as much as £30,000–40,000, but a partner

THE GOOD OLD DAYS

in a stockbroking firm would get millions, especially if he was bought by an American company, as Hoare Govett was bought by Security Pacific, or Simon & Coates by Chase Manhattan. Another essential difference was that, although the miner was told to go and look after his whippets, the stockbroker was not told to go and cultivate his garden or play golf at Sunningdale. Because it was the personnel, rather than

GOLDEN HANDCUFFS In short a financial inducement to retain a key executive. In the early days of the run-up to Big Bang it was thought that a significantly higher salary would be sufficient. Subsequently it became necessary to add hefty bonuses which would only be paid at the end of an executive's contract.

Cecil lights the fuse

PUSH

anything else, that represented the real assets of these newly acquired firms, the stockbroker was asked, nay ordered, to stay, and was given an incentive package running into hundreds of thousands of pounds. He was, however, manacled with Golden Handcuffs – the rewards were linked to a contract.

Cecil Parkinson's Big Bang

People in comfortable cartels do not willingly give them up, and Stock Exchange members showed no sign of reforming themselves to cope with the faster international world – the Americans and Japanese were not only taking all Britain's markets for real goods but were threatening to do the same with its money. A little pressure was required and Sir Gordon Borrie, the boss of the Office of Fair Trading, threatened to take the Stock Exchange to court under the Restrictive Practices Act.

As the knives came out that smooth talker Cecil Parkinson, at that time head of the Department of Trade and Industry, made a deal with Sir Nicholas Goodison, head of the Stock Exchange, that the system of fixed commissions, based on a sliding scale, would be scrapped. It was decided that, rather than have a gradual dismantling of fixed commissions, the change would take place all at once, and thereafter all dealings would be computerized.

FINANCIAL TIMES SURVEY

MONDAY
27 October
1986

THE CITY REVOLUTION

Today's Big Bang changes the London securities market irrevocably. The prize within the City's grasp is the leading position in the European time zone in a seamless market extending around the world.

BIG BANG BREAKS

The Big Day was 27 October 1986. On Saturday, 18 October, the lads held a dress rehearsal to test out the new technology, and as with most dress rehearsals some things went smoothly and others did not. To begin with, no one was sure what the proper 'dress' was, so some turned up in their smart pin-stripes as usual, others in their golfing gear. A script of imaginary deals had been given to all firms, and some people realized that if they only had so many deals to get through in the whole day they could do them all in the first hour and then go home and have that game of golf. As a result the SEAQ (Stock Exchange Automated Quota-tion) system got overloaded and broke down – a foretaste of the early days of Big Bang proper.

More ominously some market-makers (the new term for jobbers), slow to adjust their prices, were hit with sales of stock from the brokers and consequently stopped answering their telephones. Under the new rules the market-makers had to deal at the prices they were showing on the screens. But you can't deal if no one can get you on the telephone while you amend your price, can you? This was a taste of things to come. Gone were the days of dealing on the Stock Exchange floor.

Financial Times,
27 October 1986

BUYING UP THE PLAYERS

Poached and happy: Sir
Martin Jacomb moves
to Barclays

There was a time not all that long ago – well, 30 years actually – when a footballer could not be paid more than £20 a week. The flamboyant Jimmy Hill, then a player, led a strike against that restrictive practice and broke it. Thereafter players moved for ever-increasing sums to the clubs that paid them the most. The herd instinct has always been strong in the City, so they copied the footballers and set up their own transfer system, except it doesn't make the back page headlines. They added a little refinement, however – they dealt in whole teams at a time. Not long after Barclays bought the jobber Wedd Durlacher Mordaunt, for instance, eight of the newly purchased firm's senior dealers went to the merchant bankers Kleinwort Benson. It was as though the supporters at Villa Park turned up one Saturday and found eight Liverpool players in their claret and blue. They would probably be delighted – but Barclays were not, and threatened to sue (in the City of Big Bang people talked of issuing writs. They never did it, of course, but in the old days such threats would have been quite unneces-

sary. The Bank of England would have frowned and the eight players would have been back at Anfield – sorry, Barclays – before lunchtime.) In the event Barclays got their own back by poaching Sir Martin Jacomb, vice-chairman of Kleinwort, to head up its investment bank side.

The Golden Hallo

In the football world, the player transferred received up to 15% if he did not request the transfer. Tony Hateley, the father of the present England player, was transferred an enormous number of times in the sixties and was virtually able to retire on the proceeds. The City copied this too and invented a fancy name for it – the Golden Hallo. Thus as Barclays de Zoete Wedd (BZW) was losing its dealers to Kleinwort it was giving a Golden Hallo to the whole breweries research team at Fielding Newsom Smith, and then locked the Golden Handcuffs on them. Mind you, you needed to be one hell of a breweries expert to see your way clearly through the Guinness affair, which was just about to break.

One-stop shopping had come to Britain's towns and suburbs in the 1970s, but it arrived in the City on 27 October 1986. From then on you could get from any of the big new investment banks, whose activities included commercial banking, merchant banking and fund management, all the financial advice and action you needed – unit trusts and pension funds, stockbroking, and stock buying and selling. As with Sainsburys, Asda and Tesco it would all be dead efficient and cheaper. Wouldn't it?

Big Bang has certainly brought the competition which is necessary for the efficient running of any commercial activity. The Americans, and to a lesser extent the Japanese (at the moment) and the Swiss, and to an even lesser extent other foreigners, have come into the City and competed for business. As always, beware of the Japanese.

Nomura could eat Morgan Grenfell for breakfast and not even belch. The foreigners have set up shop, taken on lots of people, paid them big salaries and made them work long hours. Unfortunately there are too many of them for everyone to make a profit. In the old days people made a living, and a comfortable one – now they make a profit, or in many cases a loss. Pre-Big Bang there were six firms making a market in gilts, for instance, and the market was really dominated by two, Wedd Durlacher Mordaunt and Akroyd & Smithers. Immediately after Big Bang there were 27, and the PR companies (wait till you see what Big Bang did for PR companies) of the new conglomerates were all saying that their champion was going to capture at least 10%. Big Bang truly was a miracle if the market for gilts could expand to at least 270%.

ONE-STOP FINANCIAL SUPERMARKETS

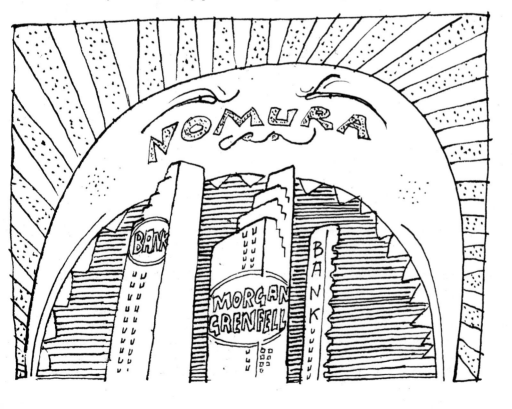

OUT WITH THE OLD...

Before the changes brought about by Big Bang it was difficult to find a non-public school type amongst the stockbroking fraternity. There were not many Oxbridge graduates, because people clever enough to get a degree there were usually clever enough to find a job more satisfying to their intellect than old-style stockbroking.

A rugby education

If your degree had effectively been gained at Twickenham or Lords that would be different, and punting shares to Buffy Cornweather and your other chums was a pretty agreeable way to spend the rest of your life, particularly if a lot of it could be done watching your successors at play. In 1971 Graham Greenwell, a senior partner at stockbroker W. Greenwell, wrote to *The Times* saying, 'The Stock Exchange is a private gentlemen's club, and not an institution which exists to perform a public service.'

In those days people would refer proudly to their stockbroker in slightly reverential terms, as though they were dropping a royal

Picking up tips at the Stock Exchange, 1951

CHARLES – THE STOCKBROKER

The younger son of our merchant banker Cecil, Charles went to Charterhouse where he achieved very little. After he didn't go to Balliol, Pater got him a job in a well-established stockbroker. He was very happy there for 20 years, looking after his clients conscientiously but never receiving the accolade of a partnership and benefiting from the financial rewards when, in the run-up to Big Bang, they sold out to an American bank. Neither the stockbroking firm nor Charles has coped very well since. He gives sound advice to his clients but cannot get to grips with the new technology and has to ask juniors to work the screens for him. Realizing that his days are numbered, he lies awake at night worrying how the school fees will be paid. He may know plenty about wines, restaurants and horses, but how are they going to be financed in the future, in spite of his private income? And his wife, who is so busy maintaining their image, has no idea what is in store when the bad news breaks.

name: 'I was chatting to my stockbroker yesterday and he was advising me to go into Cunard Steamship at six guineas.' How stockbrokers got themselves into the position where people looked up to them as professional advisers, while regarding the person who sold them a car as merely a common salesman, is one of the neatest tricks of modern times. A stockbroker is a salesman, pure and simple; probably with a posher accent than Arfur down at the Used Jalopy Mart, but none the less a salesman. He makes money if you buy or sell through him, and he doesn't if you don't.

Liberal twinges

The old fixed rate of commission allied to the huge influx of money from life assurance and pension schemes kept Charles as a stockbroker in the manner to which he had always been accustomed, and paid the school fees so that his son Henry could follow him into this 'profession' after his five years at Charterhouse. If, improbably, he ever had the remotest liberal twinge, he might once have woken up in the middle of the night wondering why such prestige accrued to such a basic job.

... IN WITH THE NEW

Equities dealing room at BZW

Brave new City

Young Henry will not become a stockbroker to follow Father's style, because Father's style has gone. (Incidentally, W. Greenwell later shed a little of its gentlemanly image and, under the ownership of the Midland Bank, bid for business so aggressively that within two years of its being taken over the Midland closed its equity division down and wiped out one of the oldest names in the City.) In this brave new City there are different types of stockbroker. In fact it is now most unlikely that someone will say he's a stockbroker. He's more likely to say, 'I work on the institutional side for BZW', or 'I'm a market-maker with Warburg.'

Henry will work in the City only if he can really sell, and if he likes the idea of working with money and for the sort of hours his father never dreamt of when he first started in the City.

The LIFFE floor

The Metal Exchange   **Brick Lane market-maker**

-2- THE MARKET-PLACE

STOCK MARKET

Equities

A stock is a share and a share is a stock. Confused? You won't be. A share is literally that: it is a 'share' in the ownership of a company. The word stock has an American flavour, but means just the same. And they're all called equities.

How is a share valued? Try this: Caffyns' shares cost 480p each and Hanson Trust's cost 138p. Caffyns is, therefore, worth three and a half times Hanson, right? Wrong. There are only 15 million Caffyns' shares in issue, so the whole company is valued at 15 million x 480 = £72 million. There are over 6,500 million shares in Hanson, capitalizing it at nearly £10 billion (6,500 million x 138) and making it about 140 times bigger than Caffyns. Companies do not always start at the same size, and they certainly do not come to the market at the same size or the same share price. The size of the company is measured by the value of the share multiplied by the number of shares issued.

You must also remember that there is a world of difference between what a company is *actually* worth and what the market *perceives* it to be worth – or what people are prepared to pay to have a stake in it. In the late sixties British Motor Holdings was producing more than a million cars a year from factories all over the country, and employing 200,000 people. In spite of all these assets BMH was valued on the stock market at less than Lesney, the company that made Matchbox toy cars.

Toys in the fast lane

The market saw BMH as an over-manned, badly managed, heavily unionized dinosaur producing poorly designed cars at a loss. It perceived Lesney as a well-managed, lean manufacturer producing well-designed products at a very great profit. The market was right about BMH – it went bust in the mid-seventies, was rescued by the taxpayer and eventually called the Rover Group, which is now to be sold to British Aerospace. But in the long run the market was wrong about Lesney, because in the early eighties it too went bust and was picked up by a Hong Kong

Small is beautiful

> **PE RATIO** Price/earnings ratio per share. PEs are calculated by dividing the company's share price by the earnings per ordinary share. In a bull market they become increasingly important as they signify how the market rates a share.

company. But there is no long run in the stock market. The people who had pushed Lesney's shares to massive heights and a ridiculous PE ratio had long gone. As the mercurial Jim Slater said, 'A good long-term investment is a short-term investment that has gone wrong.'

Yesterday's fashion

Like any crowd, the market can be ruled by its heart rather than its head. In the mid-eighties advertising agencies and PR consultancies were all the rage. The market loved them – bright, articulate, high-earning yuppies – and pushed their shares to ridiculous heights. One day a less emotional analyst noticed that the only real assets these companies had were bright, articulate, high-earning yuppies, and that the assets walked out of the door every evening. The next morning they could perfectly well be walking in through someone else's door. He advised his clients to sell, and as people began to see that the Emperor had no clothes, agencies and consultancies became yesterday's fashion.

> **FOOTSIE** The FT Stock Exchange 100 Share Index, established in 1982 to give a broader and more representative feel of the market than the FT 30 Index which had been established in 1935. The Footsie is a moving measurement of the share prices of 100 leading companies on the Stock Exchange, calculated every minute.

The power of rumour

Rumour, of course, is what moves markets. During elections, a rumour that the next opinion poll will show the Tories losing support can send the Footsie down 30 points and people can gamble on the Footsie through the traded options market. Rumours that the Department of Trade and Industry were moving in to investigate Burtons sent their shares reeling. Rumours of takeovers, rumours of oil discoveries, rumours of nickel mines, wars and rumours of wars – these constantly move share prices and make or lose fortunes.

RULED BY THE HEART

Daily Mirror, 27 May 1987

BULLS AND BEARS

BEAR A pessimist – he sells in anticipation of falling prices. **Bull** An optimist – he's an investor who buys a stock or a share in the expectation that its price will rise.

Taking tips with a pinch of salt

Tip sheets fall out of your *Investors Chronicle*, leap out of the financial pages of the *Daily Telegraph*, or pour through the post if you've ever made the mistake of sending off for some financial information. They will point out the best of the tips they have made in the past, usually telling you how you could have turned some modest investment into millions in less than five years. You are then invited to subscribe at vast expense to this learned journal which comes out monthly or weekly or both. If you have plenty of money and plenty of time to spare and plenty of pinches of salt, then fine, but remember that most of the claims made by these sheets will probably be spurious.

The tip sheets will show, for instance, how £500 would have been turned into £150,000 by buying at the very bottom and selling at the very top. They then point out that if you had put all of this £150,000 into some penny stock – a colloquial term for very low-priced shares – which they'd punted, it would have gone up ten times in no time flat and you would have ended up with £1.5 million. Simple, isn't it? And theoretically, it's just possible. But in fact you would need an incredible run of luck, and then of course it would be virtually impossible to put £150,000 into a penny stock without the price moving very sharply against you. Tip sheets proliferate in bull markets and melt like snow in Senegal in bear markets.

DARREN – THE HALF COMMISSION MAN

An 'Essex Boy', one of the new breed of half commission men, Darren's making a lot of money considering he's not 30 yet. His Mum and Dad still both work on the assembly line at an electrical component factory in Romford, and they can't understand how it is their boy's doing so well. He operates in a network of similar characters who are very alert to opportunities. You could say his teachers foresaw his brilliant future, since the only talents they remarked upon were his skill at mental arithmetic, a certain low animal cunning and a streak of opportunism.

The upwardly mobile messenger

Darren started unremarkably in the City at 15 as a filing clerk, but quickly got the sack for playing around. Then he got taken on as a stockbroker's messenger, delivering share transfer forms, which is now dealt with by computers. After that he spent several years in the back office doing routine paperwork, but he was smart enough to read the contract notes he was handling and discover who was doing the buying and selling. Soon he was placing his bets on Tricentrol and RTZ rather than Almayer's Folly and Cork Examiner in the 3.30 at Doncaster. Before long he had turned a few hundred quid into a few thousand, and had persuaded some of his mates to punt themselves. He made extra money by sharing the commission with the broker in the firm who handled his mates' deals.

The 24-year-old hits £100k

By 1980 Darren had made friends with a number of jobbers and was advising friends, relatives and even some of the partners at his firm. If you introduced a client you got 30% of the commission, and by now Darren was making more than his salary in commission. When one of the firm's dealers left he was offered his job on the Stock Exchange floor. After a year he became a blue button with an annual income of £30,000 – £12,000 salary, £12,000 commission and £6,000 bonus.

In 1987, at the height of the bull market, he left and became a half commission man with another stockbroker. Darren was confident that he would earn more from his half commission with his new firm than his final salary and commission at the old one, which was nearly £60,000. He wasn't disappointed.

> **BLUE BUTTON** A trainee stockbroker allowed to collect prices but not to transact dealings.

Darren is not one to pass up a little flutter on PA, and, kind lad that he is, he sometimes passes on a 'good tip' to one of his younger, less streetwise colleagues. The Nodecheck trick is a favourite one to play on the unsuspecting – even Darren himself got caught out in the early days.

First thing one morning a broker rang and told him about this great Swedish share.

> **PA** Personal account, an expression used by a fund manager or stockbroker to signify that he is buying or selling a share for himself and not for a client.

'Darren, I'm telling you, buy the share. It's £8.30-8.50 and definitely going to £17 by this evening.'

'Nah,' says Darren, thinking: *I've heard this before – it's the 'definitely going to be taken over at 10 o'clock tomorrow' touch.*

Three hours later the broker rings and says, 'Darren, look on your screen!'

Darren gets the price up – £12.00. *Gawd*, he thinks, but still does not buy.

Two hours later the broker rings again. Darren gets the price up again: this time it's £14. This is starting to hurt.

Five o'clock comes, the broker rings, up it comes on the screen – £17.00. Darren is almost in tears – when has he ever had such a tip?

The broker then says, 'Did you notice what time it was when I said buy?'

'No.'

'8.30. And what time is it now?'

'17.01.'

'It's the Stock Exchange clock, you twat!'

THE MARKET-MAKERS

Darren's mate Tel's job is at the sharp end – where you make the Big Money or lose it. The market-maker has one of *the* pressure jobs in the City. Tel's main interests in life are money and money, and he doesn't care who he works for as long as they pay him plenty for doing it. He's behind his screen at 8 a.m. or even 7.30, and he's on the phone constantly throughout the day.

Politics of the screen trade

There are two opposing views as to whether Tel's job is more difficult in the new City than the old. Those who think it's harder argue like this: in the old days on the Stock Exchange floor he could change a price or the amount he was prepared to deal in as the broker's dealer approached him. Now he has to post them on the screen and must deal at those prices and up to the amounts he is showing. Every computer screen in the City will have them. So if WARB is showing ICI at 978–988 50 × 50 then that means that the Warburg market-makers must be prepared to buy 50,000 ICI at 978 or sell 50,000 at 988. A rumour about oil prices could move the price sharply and could catch the market-maker out if he was holding either too much or too little stock.

The contrary view holds that the pressure is less in two significant ways. First, when the Warburg market-maker puts his prices and quantity on the screen presumably he is happy about them. If the market lurches suddenly and all the others start changing their prices, the market-maker can suddenly be unavailable on the telephone while he changes his.

'Forget this crap about not answering the phone,' says Tel. 'You don't answer the phone, you don't have a business.'

The critics respond, 'If you answer the phone when you've got a wrong price, you *will* have a loss-making business.'

NatWest won't go bust

The other reason the pressure is off, some would argue, is that the market-maker is massively capitalized compared with the old jobber. NatWest won't go bust just because their market-makers lose a few million. They might take a few scalps to show they're taking tough action, but the operation will still be there. Experienced market-makers can deal in very large amounts – though director approval, even if it's only a thumbs-up, is probably needed for anything over a £10 million trade.

Blue chips with everything: ICI's quotation on SEAQ

Tel reckons that market-makers learnt a very severe lesson in the Crash. Before, with a high volume of trading, the spreads on most shares had become dangerously narrow as too many market-makers fought

> **SHARE SPREADS** The difference between the **bid price** – what the market-maker will pay you for shares – and the **offer price** – what he will sell them to you at, i.e. his profit.

for a market share. After the Crash of 19 October 1987 spreads widened. During the Crash they became very wide, and on third and fourth lines (called gamma and delta stocks) not only did the spreads become very wide but the volumes the market-makers were prepared to deal in became derisory. On 12 October Tel was happy to deal in quarters or halves (i.e. 250,000 or 500,000) of Rotaprint and the price was 17-18p. On 19 October, when there were only sellers, the price was 4-7p and the volume was 2,500. If you had borrowed £200,000 to buy a million, as some had, you were in trouble.

Looking after the clients

In the normal course of events Tel likes to study the sector he operates in and run long of most stocks and occasionally short of some. This means he has bought stock in most of the shares in which he makes a market, but in a few he has sold stock he does not own, anticipating a fall which will enable him to buy the stock at a lower price. Tel likes to have a relationship with his clients, so that if one of them comes at him wanting 250,000 Burmah and he is short of Burmah he can ask them to go elsewhere. In return, the next time he can help them out with a point or two off the price.

RUNNING YOUR BOOK

Tel can make or lose money fast, as he did on the BP takeover of Britoil. He went short of 50,000 Britoil – i.e. sold 50,000 he hadn't got – and was just about to buy 100,000 so that he covered his 50,000 and had 50,000 in hand, when some fuckwit in the dealing room shouted: 'Dawn raid on Britoil!' and the price shot ahead a full pound. Lovely for Tel – he has to tell the other market-maker he's plugged into! Actually many would not have, but Tel has been around for 20 years and is straight, and he therefore passes up £100,000 profit. Ouch. Worse still, he has to cover the 50,000 he is short, and lose £1 on each one. 'It's happened before. Next time the luck'll go my way,' he shrugs.

Someone else's money

Tel does not deal for PA. He would need permission in writing to do so, and anyway he feels that having his own shares would

> **DAWN RAID** If your company is the subject of a dawn raid it means that another company has bought a substantial number of your shares from one or several institutions before anyone has realized what is happening.

affect his judgement. He wants to concentrate from 7.15 to 6.30 on running his book. At 6.30 he hands it over to a colleague who runs the late shift to cope with New York. The next day he might need to buy 100,000 Glaxo that he'd sold the night before on Wall Street. Because he thought Glaxo would open lower, and they did – 15p – he made a nice start to the day with a profit of £15,000. However, if the *FT* had been bullish about Glaxo he might have had to pay 20p more than the price at which he'd sold, and the day would have started with a £20,000 loss.

Studying the form

I'M LISTENING TO MYSELF SELLING PATTERSON SOME DUD CORN FUTURES LAST WEDNESDAY.

Taping the evidence

Most telephone deals in the City are tape recorded. Tel grins delightedly as he remembers one call in particular.

'What about that time, Darren, when you was taped when you'd been chatting up that bird?'

Darren had been selling 10,000 shares to a girl called Julie who worked in one of the other brokers. While discussing the sale they were also talking about holidays, and Julie said she'd just come back from St Tropez.

'Yeah, that's right,' said Darren. 'I seen you there – what a great pair of tits.' Amidst all this excitement Julie marked the sale as 5,000 and Darren as 10,000. Inevitably a query came up and Julie, forgetting the glandular references in the conversation, listened to the tape with one of her directors. There was some embarrassment.

Like everything else in the City the cost of taping doesn't come cheap. The machines can record up to 64 lines simultaneously and cost £35,000 each. A 24-hour tape costs £50. When you think that some of the institutions have over 1,500 telephone lines you can see where the money goes.

Tel listens unsmiling to Darren talking about a recent incident concerning a disagreement between a broker and a market-maker which was only solved because the broker had also taped the conversation. It concerned the sale of 50,000 shares in a volatile stock which had fallen sharply after the sale. The next day there was a query from the department matching the bargains, as the broker's note was in but there was no matching note from the market-maker. When the broker contacted the market-maker, he denied all knowledge of the bargain. The broker therefore insisted on listening to the market-maker's tapes – all

DON'T KILL THE BUSINESS

Sir Nicholas Goodison: a good fairy to the market-makers?

market-makers' conversations are recorded. When he listened to them there was no sign of the bargain. Luckily for him and unluckily for the market-maker who had erased the conversation, the broker had taped it himself.

Some of the new regulations, too, may well kill the business, they think. Threats of doing away with the account and imposing seven-day settlements come in for a lot of stick.

'We need the account punters,' says Tel. 'They get the market going and then the institutions come in 'cos they think they're missing something. That Goodison, he's all

right but doesn't want to let the regulations boys go too far. Mind you, I thought it was well out of order when the boys marked the price of TSB down when it was announced he was the new chairman.'

> **THE ACCOUNT** The Stock Exchange year is divided into 25 account periods, usually two weeks long but sometimes three, with a specific settlement day for payment a few days after each account. **Buying shares 'for the account'** means buying and selling them within the Stock Exchange account, so no capital has to be put up.

BEASTIE – THE TWO-PHONE FIXER

Like Darren, Beastie is a half commission man. Beastie doesn't think about evil one way or the other. He doesn't really think much at all, except about money, and clients for whom he could produce money, and who therefore produce it for him.

Recently he was dealing with two of his biggest clients, both of whom were heavily involved in big takeovers. One of their three-way phone conversations, Beastie with a phone at each ear, would have made a DTI inspector's hair curl.

'George, I'm in touch with Oscar Schreiber. He'd like you to buy some of his shares.'

'Why, Beastie?'

'Because he's involved in this takeover and he needs his share price supported. He needs buyers.'

'But I don't want to buy his fucking shares, Beastie.'

Beastie now talks out of the left hand side of his mouth as opposed to his right. 'Mr Ince doesn't seem very keen to buy any of your shares, Mr Schreiber.'

'Tell Mr Ince there's something in it for him.'

The cigarette rolls back to the other side of his mouth. 'George, he says there's something in it for you.'

'Like what, shm … Mr Schreiber?'

'Like £10 million.'

Beastie's eyes flicker slightly.

'£10 million, George.'

'What have I got to do for £10 million quid, Beastie?'

'What would you like him to do, Mr Schreiber?'

'I'd like him to buy £50 million of my shares.'

'He'd like you to buy 50 big ones, George.'

'I bet he fucking would, Beastie. Tell him to get lost.'

'He says he's not too keen, Mr Schreiber.'

'Tell him I'll guarantee him against any loss.'

'He'll guarantee you against any loss, George.'

'If the schmuck is going to pay me £10 million, what about my costs?'

'Mr Schreiber, Mr Ince is worried about his costs.'

'Tell him I'll pay those too.'

'He'll pay those, George.'

'Are you sure this is all kosher, Beastie?'

'This is all perfectly legal, isn't it, Mr Schreiber?'

'It's legal. I have been assured by City advisers of considerable eminence.'

'It's kosher, George.'

'OK, tell the schmuck I'll buy his lousy shares and make sure his £10 million is here tomorrow – and no messing.'

CHARLOTTE – THE RESEARCH ANALYST

Roedean-educated Charlotte went into the City at the age of 21, straight from one of the nicer provincial universities. She had no particular motivation except that she wanted status and a smart lifestyle. Her provincial bank manager father and his wife had scrimped and saved to pay their children's school fees. The resultant no-frills austerity at home, combined with the bracing South Downs air in termtime, had fired Charlotte with a fierce will to succeed and to make the world see that she had done so. Little did she know how easy it would prove to be!

Her first job was as a research assistant at a small stockbroker who paid her about the same as a secretary, but with a pleasant 40% bonus on top. Two undemanding years later Charlotte moved on to a more established firm of stockbrokers, as a junior investment analyst on a team specializing in retail stores such as Debenhams, Burtons and W.H. Smith. The operative word was 'team', and in the early eighties poaching and team transfers were the quickest way to raise your salary and status. After three team transfers Charlotte, now all of 27, is working for an American group where her salary, bonus and very generous perks make up a 'remuneration package' worth about £100,000. The major embarrassment to this Child of Big Bang is that she earns (sorry, gets paid) about four times as much as her hard-working father.

The Beasties of this world don't need to consult investment analysts like Charlotte. Beastie has his way of earning loadsa money, but what does Charlotte do to pick up her £100,000 per annum? Not a lot. She gets to work at 7.45 – prices have started to change on the screens from about 7.30 – and has a morning meeting with the rest of her team, which consists of two analysts and two salesmen. They will discuss the action for the day – 'Shall we try and persuade our clients to change into Boots from Marks & Spencer?'.

The reason they want to do this is because the team needs to earn £2.5 million in commission (i.e. five times their combined remuneration of £500,000) and they therefore need to persuade their clients to switch their investments as well as making new ones. The clients are fund managers at merchant banks, insurance companies and pension funds. After the meeting is over Charlotte will try and talk to the key people at Marks and at Boots.

The rest of the morning passes pleasantly enough in a little desk research into the major players in the stores sector. Charlotte does not bother with the minor players. What's the point? Even if she finds out that they are going places, the market in the shares is so small that her clients would scarcely be interested. Charlotte has not yet been around long enough to hear the dictum 'Accumulate quietly'.

The glamour of supermarkets

At this stage she should perhaps have a word with John Hewitt, the chief executive of Scrimgeour Vickers, the stockbroker absorbed with some difficulty by the American bank Citicorp. Twenty years ago when John, fresh down from Oxford, was doing the equivalent job to Charlotte's on a salary of £950 (a year, not a week), he

discovered a little company called Associated Dairies. They were small even in the dairy world, but being a thorough and well-read chap he noticed that their annual report mentioned an investment in a supermarket company. Supermarkets, believe it or not, were the glamour stock of the day – they were either terrific, like Tesco, or went bust, like Brierleys. John went to see Associated Dairies with one of the investment managers at the Pru. They decided that the company was either going bust or it was the cheapest stock on the market. It was the latter – £10,000 in Asda in 1965 would now be worth £2 million. It made Hewitt's reputation.

John Hewitt: Associated Dairies made him, Citicorp got him

SERIOUS RESEARCH

PETER – THE PRIVATE PUNTER

In his early forties, happily married with three sons, Peter is a public school and minor Oxbridge college product. As you might imagine, he plays golf. He's not directly involved in the City, but he *is* fascinated by it. He pores over the *Financial Times* and the City pages of the serious nationals. Managing director of his own company, he can usually lay his hands on the equivalent of about £50,000 for speculation, and over the years he has made some awful boobs though he has had the odd success. He believes that his major handicap is lack of inside information; in fact it's late information and lack of bottle. Peter is a devout Thatcherite. His heart and mind are in the right place, but he's no match for the Darrens who bask lazily in the warm waters lapping the City shores.

Peter can't afford Charlotte's services, but has learnt enough about the market over the years to know that you can make money in bear markets just as you can in bull markets. He has never done so himself because like a rabbit in a car's headlights he becomes paralyzed when prices fall and holds on to shares he has bought because he thinks the market is treating them unfairly. As he bought them at 168, they must be wildly undervalued at 107.

Too clever by half

He once tried to sell short – he was in the West Car Park at Twickenham when one of his friends from the Midlands told him that Crompton Parkinson, the light bulb manufacturers, were going bust. The price was 25p and Peter saw the chance to make a quick killing. First thing on Monday he rang Charles, his broker, and sold 10,000.

> **SELLING SHORT** Selling shares you don't own in the hope of buying them back cheaper later on.

'Fine,' said Charles, who knew that Peter didn't have any Crompton Parkinson shares. It's not strictly illegal to sell shares you don't own, but it is frowned upon. Peter was delighted to get the 25p price – he thought he might only get 23p. All he had to do now was to wait for Crompton Parkinson to turn the lights out as they left the building, and he could mop up 10,000 of the bankrupt stock at a nominal 2p, giving himself a nice little earner of around £2,300. Not bad for a Saturday afternoon, even if England had lost again. On Tuesday he was flabbergasted when he read in his *Standard* that Thorn had made a bid, and the price was now 125p. There was no way out. He had to buy 10,000 at 125p to cover his sale. His bright idea at

Twickenham had cost him over £10,000 in 24 hours.

Thin markets

When you read in the *FT* market report that Dares Estates rose sharply in a thin market, or more ominously that Acorn fell sharply in a thin market, what does it mean? Many private investors found out the hard way in October 1987. They had bought all the hyped shares of the previous few months – Blacks Leisure, Property Trust, Rotaprint, Eagle Trust. Peter had found no trouble in buying, though in retrospect it was irritating having to pay 18p for 50,000 Rotaprint when the price in the paper had shown 15p. But what was 3p when the price would be a pound by Christmas?

19 October. Crash. Whoops. Maybe Peter should sell those Rotaprint. They were, after all, a bit speculative. He rang Charles, his broker, and asked him to sell them. The price in the *FT* was 15p but he was prepared to lose £1,500; after all, he had made several thousands during the year. He was, however, slightly stunned when Charles phoned half an hour later – he had had some trouble in getting through to his dealer – and told him that he could sell 1,000 at 12p or 2,000 at 10p. There was no chance of selling 50,000. Peter learnt quickly what he now vaguely remembered reading – for a seller there has to be a buyer. Just because it says in the *FT* that the price is 15p it does not mean you will get, say, 14p, and it certainly does not mean you will get it for 50,000 shares. At least he now knows what a thin market is.

'Oh, well,' said Peter, 'I'll hang on. They'll come back.'

Blooper. That was his second mistake. Rotaprint called in the Receiver in February 1988, and the shares which only last Sep-tember were definitely going to £1 went to nothing. One consolation: Peter can carry forward his £9,500 loss to offset against the capital gains we're sure he's going to make in the future.

Penny shares

Bearing in mind what can happen to marketability in small stocks, known now as gamma and delta stocks, is it worth invest-ing in penny shares? The temptation is strong. Over the years Peter has been tempted into them for two reasons. First, you get lots for your money. He got 50,000 Rotaprint shares for just over £9,000. If he had put £9,000 into ICI instead, he would only have got 600 shares. Secondly, no one told him – and if they had he wouldn't have believed them – that ICI was going to £100, whereas he was told by several people that Rotaprint was going to 100p.

Emotionally, to satisfy Peter's greed, it had to be Rotaprint. Logically, it should have been ICI. ICI will reach £100 before Rotaprint reaches 100p. After all, now that Rotaprint is in the cemetery ICI has for ever to do it.

PRIVATE PITFALLS

Private punters watching the Crash of '87 at Debenhams

FROM RAGS TO RICHES

Thrills and frills: investors in the scrum for Laura Ashley shares

But one day Peter will make money on a penny stock. He could have been, but wasn't, in former rag trade company Polly Peck. If he had bought 50,000 in 1980 they would have cost him £2,000. If he had held them for a few months, when the price went from 4p not just to £1 but to £3, his holding would have been worth £150,000. If he had resisted the temptation to sell and held on for two years, when the price rose to £35, his original £2,000 would have become a staggering £1.75 million. Peter was mildly irritated, as we all are, by missing such an opportunity, but he felt better when he was chatting in the men's bar at the RAC to a friend. The friend told him that he had bought 25,000 Polly Peck at 6½p. Peter was just going green when he finished the sentence – 'and I sold them next day at 7¼p.' No one ever went broke taking a profit, as they say, but you can miss out on £875,000.

How to become a stag

By the summer of 1987 we were all becoming stags. With British This and British That being offered at X, and always opening on day one at X plus 30, a stag was the thing to be. A stag was certain of his profit, or felt he was. It was a sure-fire way to make money. Wasn't it?

> **STAG** Someone who buys a new issue and then sells it quickly for a short-term profit.

When a company offers its shares to the public it is not axiomatic that Peter will rush out and buy them. If he doesn't the issue flops, and many of the shares are left with the underwriters – those institutions who agree to take them whatever happens. The price drops and everyone is unhappy. Even in the raging bull market of 1986-7 there were flops – the beautiful Mrs Fields and her cookies, the efficient GT Management and the high-profile Morgan Grenfell all spring to mind.

To make any pretence at making serious money as a stag you have to devote quite a lot of time and effort to it. You could start by getting some essential preliminaries in place, like two bank accounts: one in town for the fast clearance of received cheques, and one out of town – Scunthorpe, perhaps – for the slower clearance of your own cheques. Interest charges can be a significant cost. You also need to have arranged a decent overdraft facility, say £50,000 or £100,000 – better still £500,000 – with your local bank manager. If you are a stag you must sell as soon as dealings start. Stay in longer and you're not a stag, you're an investor. But how do you know your allocation if the allotment letter hasn't arrived by the time dealings start? You ring your bank the day before and find out if your cheque has been presented. If it has, then you have been allocated some shares and you will know from the public announcement of allocation how many your level of application will have received. To make the effort worthwhile, multiple applications have to be allowed, and you've got to be in there with the Best of them. Watch it if they're not.

Looking after your friends

We will shortly see what a pig's breakfast the government and Lazards made of the Britoil issue, but perhaps one of the reasons criticism was so muted was because the lads have been doing roughly the same thing for years. If Cazenove, they of the legendary placing power, were sponsoring a new issue they would make damn sure their friends received a goodly chunk of stock before Peter ever got near his puny 150 after applying for 5,000. If the issue was a real winner, and the press joined in the hype, he might not even get the 150 as there would be a ballot. Peter would then have sent a cheque for probably £10,000 on which he either loses or pays interest, according to his liquidity position. This money will be held for at least two weeks earning interest for someone else (guess who?), and he might get 150 shares which could go to a premium of 30p. Peter now has a gross profit of £45 from which he must deduct his bank charges of £46 (two weeks at 12% on £10,000) and, if he wants to sell, a minimum broker's commission of £25 plus VAT = £28.75. So, having got all enthused about Arlington Securities or Capital Radio, and having been delighted to have been allocated some

shares, and having guessed correctly that the shares would go to a premium, Peter has lost £29.75 – what a clever little stag he is!

Leave stagging to the professionals who have got the time and the liquid resources. To make money you want to be punting for £50,000 or £100,000 so that you finish up with a few thousand.

Gilts

An extremely important area of the stock market consists of dealing in British government bonds, more popularly known as 'gilts'. Such bonds are simply government IOUs guaranteeing the investor a flow of interest payments and capital repayment at a predetermined date. Whereas risk is always inherent in the price movement of shares in the equity market, bonds have a guarantee of repayment in the future. Unless, of course, you were unlucky enough to have invested in Barlow Clowes International, thinking that Peter Clowes would only be dealing in the gilt market.

FROM RICHES TO RAGS

Long arm of the law: Peter Clowes is escorted into Bishopsgate police station

HOW TO BUY THE CHANCE TO BUY

An empty future: only traded options are dealt in at the Stock Exchange now

Options

Option dealing in shares is part of the Stock Exchange, and when Peter reads this book he will want to emulate Darren and make money out of traded options. Before he does that he will need to learn about traditional options. A traditional option is an option to buy or sell a certain number of shares at a certain price by a certain date in the future, usually three months ahead. In many ways traded and traditional options are very similar – the idea is the same, gearing up, but in operation they are very different. The market in traded options is relatively new and was only set up some ten years ago. Dealing in them actually still takes place on the floor of the Stock Exchange in Throgmorton Street – the lone survivors after Big Bang when dealing in equities, gilts and traditional options was transferred to offices and screens.

There is one vital word missing from traditional options, and that is 'traded'. There is no market in traditional options. Once Peter has that option he can only do two things with it – exercise it or abandon it. He cannot trade it on the market. Secondly, whereas traded options can only be done in a limited number of major shares, a couple of gilts, the Footsie and one or two currencies, traditional options can be set up in almost any stock, not only on the London Stock Exchange but throughout the world.

> **GEARING UP** Increasing the impact of your capital by putting up only a percentage of your investment.

Traditional Options

To start with, Peter must be convinced that a share is going to move quite sharply one way or the other within three months. It is no good if it moves a bit – he cannot trade the option – and it is no good taking a twelve-month view – he only has three months. Let's take our old friend Polly Peck. Peter missed out on its rise from 6p to £3 but he was convinced it would fly again. He rang his broker and the price, in this case the striking price, was £3.05. For an option he had to pay 31p, i.e. just over 10%. In most shares the option price will be about 10%, though in volatile shares it can be 15 or 20%. In biggies like ICI it can be only 7½%.

CALL OPTION This confers the right to buy a fixed number of shares at a specified price within a predetermined period of time. **Put option** This allows you to sell a fixed number of shares under the same conditions.

EXERCISE PRICE The price at which the buyer or seller of an option may buy or sell the underlying security.

Peter wanted to invest £2,000 and he was therefore able to give a call to buy 6,000 Polly Peck any time in the following three months (6,000 × 31p). If he had bought the shares he would have only been able to buy about 600 with the same money. We must now track some theoretical movements of the share price before coming back to what actually happened. If in the next three months Peter had got it completely wrong and the Polly Peck price declined, say to 270, there would be no point in exercising his option – buying the 6,000 at his striking price of 305 – to sell them at 270 because he would lose £2,100, so he might as well just let his option lapse and lose his £2,000 instead. If he had bought the shares he would be showing a £210 paper loss (600 × 35p), but he would at least have his shares and could choose whether to take the small loss or hold on for recovery.

If, however, the shares rose a little, say to 325, it would have been worth Peter's while to exercise the option – he could, after all, buy at 305 and sell at 325 – but he would still have lost money. The option money is a *non-returnable deposit*. In this example, if he had bought the shares he would be showing a small profit of £120 (600 × 20p), which he could either take by selling the shares or run by holding on to them.

Peter gets it right

But we all know what actually happened. Peter was right. Polly Peck took off again and went all the way to £35, though not in three months – and remember we only have three months. In that time they went to £12. So what happened to Peter's £2,000? On the option front he exercised his right to buy 6,000 at 305, sold at £11.95 and pocketed 6,000 × £8.90 = £53,400, less his £2,000 option money (which by the way he had to pay on the nail three months earlier), and being Peter he wondered what to do with it. If he had bought the shares he would be sitting on 600 worth £12 each, and if he sold them he would be showing a profit of £5,400, still damn good but not the spectacular return the option gave him. Options effectively gear you up 10 to 1. Once you have passed break-even – i.e. the share price rises or falls by more than 10%, or actually nearer 12% with costs – you will make ten times as much as you would by buying the shares. But they have to move substantially, and within three months, or, as Peter usually does, you lose.

THE LOW RISK ROUTE

HOW TO TURN £10,000...

Sophisticated humour is a notable characteristic among traded option dealers

Traded Options

We know Darren is a successful half commission man. We have also seen that Peter has been a straightforward investor for many years – since his father sold his business in the Midlands, in fact, and passed on some of the proceeds to avoid death duty.

In the spring of 1987 Peter was convinced by the financial commentators he read that the £ would rise against the $. In addition he played golf with a friend from the Department of Trade and Industry who, although not willing or able to speculate himself, was pretty sure that that was likely to be the case. Completely convinced, Peter decides to invest £10,000.

He buys sterling 'forward' at the $1.50 rate. To his great delight he watches the polls more and more confidently predicting a Tory victory in the election, bringing a rise in the value of the £ with each poll. He sells in May when the £ has reached a value of $1.65. He has made 15 cents on $1.50, i.e. 10%, in two months; £1,000 is not at all bad, and Peter is feeling pretty pleased with himself. He buys drinks all round at the golf club, and a case of Glenfiddich.

At the same time Darren, with slightly less hard information than Peter has had access to, feels that the £ is rising against the $ and senses that it has further to go. Darren is not interested in a 10% profit. He wants to make serious money. On the currency traded options market he can buy options to buy pounds at various rates and for various months. He can buy, say, March $1.50s, April $1.55s or May $1.60s. Being the gambler he is, Darren decides to go for the May $1.60s which, with the £ currently at

> **OUT-OF-THE-MONEY   OPTION**
> A call option whose exercise price is above the current price of the underlying security.

$1.50, means that he is 10 cents 'out of the money'. Note that he has bought an option. He has not bought pounds and has no intention of doing so. His gamble is that, if his hunch about the rising £ is correct, a big institution or a big corporation will be glad to buy a large number of pounds in May at several cents less than the then ruling price. That is what gives options their value.

So Darren has bought an option to buy pounds at $1.60 per pound in May. Remember that it's now March, and the rate is $1.50. For that option he pays 0.2 cents per unit (the price, after all, has to rise 10 cents before he reaches break-even, and that rise has to come by the middle of May). For his £10,000 he can buy 600 contracts (a contract is 12,500 units) so 12,500 x 0.2 cents = $250 x 600 = $15,000 = £10,000.

By early May the rate has moved to $1.65, and the option is worth 5 cents (it has gone over $1.60 to $1.65) plus a little in case it goes any further in the rest of May, say 0.5 cent. The option is now worth 5.5 cents instead of the 0.2 cents Darren paid for it, and his 600 contracts are worth 600 x 12,500 x 5.5 cents = $412,500 = £250,000. He has turned his £10,000 investment into £250,000 in just two months.

While Peter buys lunch at Royal Lytham, Darren buys a new Porsche and flies to Marbella to negotiate the purchase of that apartment he and his girlfriend want.

The naked accountant

Most people never dabble in the traded options market at all. Those who do usually confine themselves to buying call or put options where the most they can lose is their original stake. But for someone to buy an option, someone else has to sell or 'write' the option. The writer can either be 'covered', i.e. he owns the underlying security of the option he is selling, or he can be 'naked' – he does not own it. Writing covered options is not very risky, because the worst that can happen is the forced sale of the underlying security. But the writing of uncovered options can be very risky indeed if the market swings violently. On Black Monday and the next day the market dropped so far so fast that anyone who had written put options – anyone who had reckoned the market would be going up, not down – was in serious trouble.

Enter a trainee accountant, a client of County Nat West. He managed to lose a million quid. How could he have done it? Try this as a possibility: supposing he had

> **FOOTSIE 2250 SERIES** In the traded options market it is possible to speculate on movements in the FT Stock Exchange 100 Index – the Footsie. The marks used for trading are in steps of 50, i.e. 2200, 2250, 2300, 2350. In the week before the Crash the Footsie level was just over 2300 and if you were confident it would not fall you would sell options at 2250.

sold puts on the October Footsie 2250 series, which rose from 15p to 450p in two days. Each contract therefore would have risen from £150 to £4,500 and he would have had to find £4,350 for each contract he had written. Most people, if they do stray into the option writing market, are satisfied with gambling on one or two contracts. But our friend, buoyed up by his continual successes in writing puts (it is, after all, a sure-fire way to make money in a bull market), could well have enthusiastically written 250 contracts. He would, therefore, have had to find 250 × 4,350 = £1,087,500.

...INTO £250,000 IN EIGHT WEEKS

THE DEAD CAT BOUNCE

The irony is that if the market Crash had come just 72 hours later, the trainee would have made a nice little profit of £37,500 instead of his loss – the contracts expired on the Wednesday. On the other hand if the Crash had happened the week before he would have lost an even more impressive £1.5 million as the market continued to fall. In the options market timing is everything.

As if it was not bad enough finding you had given a 23-year-old trainee accountant a £1 million line of credit, County NatWest then discovered that one of its equity salesmen had also been playing the options market and lost not just one but *three* big ones. To add a little spice to the operation the salesman, because he was not supposed to trade PA, had punted through his father, a worm breeder from Fife in Scotland. Having lost a packet when the Crash came – having written or sold put options – he then wrote calls into the recovery, the classic Dead Cat Bounce. NatWest discovered it – they even had recorded tapes of the transaction inexorably taking place – put a stop to it and faced losses of £3 million. They certainly know now what the Dead Cat Bounce means. Rumour has it that if the positions had been allowed to run – after all, the Dead Cat dropped again – the £3 million would have been clawed back. Maybe, reply NatWest, but if the Dead Cat had bounced higher we might have lost £6 million.

Greedy young bucks

NatWest were not the only ones to employ young bucks who displayed greed, fear and ego in equal measure. Smith New Court unearthed two of its traded options dealers who between them had lost over £4 million for their employer. Options punting can be like horse racing – the temptation is to keep betting, in bigger and bigger money. You're bound to be right sooner or later. In the world of 1987, when everyone was making pots of money, it took a real man to admit he had lost.

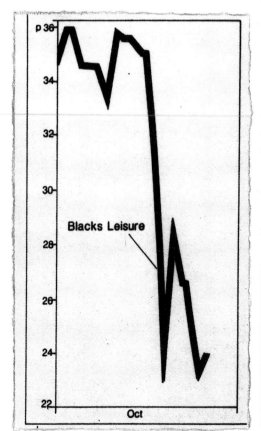

The bounce of an unlucky black cat, Black's Leisure (*Investors Chronicle*)

DEAD CAT BOUNCE If you drop a cat from the top of the NatWest Tower, it will bounce first before falling back to the ground – dead. Similarly if market prices drop sharply from a great height they bounce up, before dropping again, largely because people who sold short have to buy back to complete the transaction.

Money Market

The money market is the vehicle for the flow of short-term money in the banking system, and because it rarely deals with the general public, little is understood about it. Money brokers operate in a world of domestic and cross-border leveraged leasing, of project finance and tax-advantaged equity and debt placements. In a booklet which attempts to explain what they do, one firm of money brokers talk of their services in these words: 'Our highly experienced team of professionals handle all standard money market instruments, including domestic deposits, Euro-sterling deposits, certificates of deposit, FRAs, interest rate swaps, and options including caps and collars.' No kidding!

Live fast, die young

Money brokers also talk into their phones and at each other in a quite indecipherable language:

'Lightning, you got anything long-end CDs?'

'You ought to get on at half seven-sixteenths.'

'I made him a half seven – agreed?'

'I sell at seven NatWest 5 million one year.'

'I'll sell a plonker at same.'

'I'm a buyer at a half for Salomon.'

'Mine at 7.'

'How much at 7, Tone?'

'Two handfuls.'

'Blow his tits off.'

Mind you, it's all taken deadly seriously, and Lightning and his pals can earn serious money – £100,000 plus. They get up early and get in early, having read the papers, listened to the radio, looked at Reuters, Knight Rider and Telerate. They work at their contacts and they play in big numbers. They age prematurely and die young.

SELLING A PLONKER

'Blow his tits off!': secret language of money broking

RAMBO STERLING WIMPY DOLLAR

Foreign Exchange Market

In contrast to the money market the foreign exchange market is very much in everyone's mind, from Peter buying currency for his foreign holiday to news of whether the $ is strong or weak against the £ and so on. A lot of speculative, rather than investment, buying takes place in this market.

Pounds, dollars, deutschmarks, yen, francs – they are in the end only a means of exchange. The reason their value in relation to each other changes is because countries' rates of inflation vary and so they print their currencies in differing volumes. If Britain prints more pounds it does not become any wealthier; there are just more pieces of paper around to make up that wealth. Each piece of paper is therefore worth a little bit less and the £ should gradually depreciate against other currencies.

However, to make international trade

A cock-up at the Bank

easier a system of relating currencies to each other has been devised. Only when it becomes obvious that one country is inflating faster than others does everyone start to avoid that currency, or sell whatever they have of it, and the currency changes its relationship to the others – sometimes sharply. Confidence in a country's stability also plays a part, though even this is tied up with inflation because instability nearly always means inflation – i.e. the gradual or sharp debasement of a currency. Thus the South African rand is currently weak because of the instability in the country.

Locking into the dollar

In the international trading of money that permeates the City the value of the leading currencies is of paramount importance. As with every other financial instrument in the City, there are markets in all the currencies – both for those who genuinely need them because they need to buy dollars or yen or deutschmarks for their business, and for those who want to speculate in them. For example Jaguar cars, whose share price appears to have become locked into the $, uses the financial futures market constantly. It hedges its dollar sales by buying forward. Assuming Jaguar wants £15,000 for every car it sells to the USA, then in early 1985, when the £ bought $1.10, it was selling the cars for $16,500. By early 1988, however, the exchange rate had changed dramatically. The £ was buying $1.90 and to get their £15,000 Jaguar was having to sell at $28,500 – quite a difference even to rich Americans, particularly when the extra $12,000 had received the various mark-ups through the selling chain. Jaguar can either put its $ prices up or take less than £15,000. Hopefully, however, it saw the swing coming and some time in 1986 sold its dollars forward when the rate was better than $1.90.

Eurobond Market

There are 500,000 workers in the City, even if there are only 20,000 who sleep there by night. There are only a few hundred Eurobond salesmen, but they are the boys with the big salaries, the red Porsches and the £500,000 flats in Kensington.

What is a Eurobond? It is a relatively new animal, and it developed from the desire of Americans not to repatriate dollars to the USA in the sixties for tax reasons. This led to the Eurodollar and on to the Euroyen and the ECU or European Currency Unit. The Eurobond market became large and sophisticated with everyone getting in there – multinationals, large corporations, even governments.

The tombstone

The 'tombstone' ad in the *Financial Times* or the *Wall Street Journal* is the first that most investors will learn about a new issue. It is called a tombstone because of its shape and dullness, and it will tell you, for instance, that Ronson's Heron Group has issued ECU 60m. 9⅜ guaranteed retractable bonds repayable between 1992 and 1997. The bonds will be 'unconditionally guaranteed jointly and severally by Heron International NV of Curaçao in the Netherlands Antilles and Heron International plc of London'. Underneath this will be a list of banks from Britain, America, Europe and Japan, and above it the names of three other banks. All this tells you that the three banks had organized the raising of the capital and the others had guaranteed to find buyers.

One advantage to a large corporation is its tax efficiency, helped by a subsidiary in Luxembourg or the Netherlands Antilles (*Private Eye* thinks Gerald Ronson might get a knighthood there even if he's muffed his chances of one here). Another advantage is the easy switching of the money raised to any part of the world, but the major advantage is anonymity. There is no central register, and this prevents anyone probing to discover the bondholder's titanic wealth and maybe taxing it a little.

Stepdown floater

This is where our Eurobond salesman comes in. He's a high-pressure salesman, but he also has to know his clients and what type of bond might fit their investment needs. It's no good trying to sell a heaven and hell bond to a client who wants a bull and bear one, or a zebra to someone who wants a stepdown floater, even if he knows what the hell the bloke's talking about. He is dealing in megabucks so Peter will not feature in his Psion Organizer.

SECRET WEALTH

THE SWEET TASTE OF SUGAR

Commodity Market

Darren's pal Ricky, another Essex Boy, works in the commodity futures market at FOX (Futures and Options Exchange) on Commodity Quay by St Katharine's Dock. It's just down the road from the old Spitalfields market, and a fair number of the sons of the old potato traders there are now potato futures traders. Ricky's now over 40 and working for himself, having been employed over the years by several of the commodity dealers. He's what's known as a 'local', trading for himself primarily in the sugar market though he can move on to the trading floors nearby: coffee, cocoa, oil, options.

At FOX trading still takes place just as it has for decades, with the dealers on the floor shouting out their bids and offers and waving their arms to show whether they are buyers or sellers. These days, of course, the telephones and computers are in there too.

London loses its place

FOX emerged in 1987 as a more marketing-oriented operation than its parent, the old London Commodity Exchange, and moved from Plantation House to a purpose-built exchange where its market floor is shared by the International Petroleum Exchange. It's going to need its marketing approach – London has lost its place as the centre of the commodity market, which is now dominated by New York.

Ricky earned himself a bit of a reputation in the market in 1980 when he worked out that the price of sugar was set to rise, and sharply. His view was confirmed when he visited the US Department of Agriculture in Washington and met a Cuban exile. This exile told him he went backwards and forwards to Cuba (a very important producer of sugar), and Ricky realized he was a bit more than just an exile. Nevertheless he was surprised when his contact produced a load of satellite photographs showing that the Cuban sugar crop had rust disease.

Not for the faint-hearted

Ricky knew for certain then that his analysis was right. The market was going to be short of physical product and the price was going to rise. For his firm, though not for himself, he bought thousands of lots – one lot is 50 tonnes – both physical and terminal. ('Terminal' is speculative paper, whereas 'physical' is the actual product, or 'actuals'.) So did the US and Soviet governments – they can work out what their satellite photographs mean too. The price rose from $105 a tonne to over $400, and they all made a stack of money.

As a 'local' Ricky can now take advan-

The price is right: gas-oil dealers press their buttons in a trading pit on Commodity Quay

tage of such a situation himself – except that capital and either real guts or real stupidity, depending on how you view it, are needed to make a real killing. He likes to close his position – he owes no money and is owed none – each day so that he can sleep at night. This example of a deal he did will show you why.

He received an order to buy 6,000 lots of sugar at a price of $200 a tonne (6,000 × 50 × $200 = $60 million). Now he knows that such buying will push the price up so he can afford – or thinks he can – to buy for his own company say 500 lots at $205. He therefore does this for his firm. Then he gets on with the big order and that weight of buying pushes the price up to $215 a tonne. He then sells his firm's 500 tonnes and shows them a profit of 500 × 50 × $10 = $250,000, thank you very much.

That looks easy, doesn't it? And usually it is. But one thing could have happened. The big buyer could have cancelled his order after he had bought the 500 lots for his firm and the price could have fallen below the $200. The commodity market is not for faint hearts.

The bastard category

There are three types of commodity broker. The first is the broker who actually trades the physical commodity and uses the futures market as an essential tool to hedge the risks for his customers. He will deal, for example, with an Australian farmer who might want to sell the crop which he hasn't even planted yet in order to generate some cash flow. The second is the speculator operating the market as an investment tool. The third is the bastard who takes innocent, though stupid, private investors for a ride.

The bastard category have various techniques and the following is typical. About 30 fast-talking, well-spoken young men are recruited – the accent is crucial: we can't have Ricky's voice trying to convince a nice old lady to stump up another £5,000 to protect her first £5,000. They are given a week's intensive training on how the futures market operates, and then set to work.

To recruit the suckers – sorry, investors – mail-shots would be used extensively with all the tired old Open Me gimmicks such as 'You have already won a Major Prize.' Anyone daft enough to reply would then be written down as a legitimate target and would receive a telephone call. This first call would be extremely laid-back and

RECRUITING THE SUCKERS

GET THAT MONEY IN

gentle, in well-modulated public school tones. It would seek to establish exactly how much time the victim was worth and would also talk of the fabulous money to be made by dealing with the big boys in the world of oil and platinum and Treasury notes. Many of the people who want to invest in commodities do it because it brings excitement to their humdrum life as a suburban housewife or a lower management dogsbody.

Bear in mind when you are trading in commodity futures that, although theoretically you might be buying thousands of barrels of oil or tons of copper, they are unlikely to land on your doorstep, because you sell them before they do. Also, you may well ask, how do you buy so much gear with so little money? Margins are the answer to commodity trading. You only have to put up a small percentage of the total cost of the thousands of barrels of oil. The way you make – or lose – a large percentage of your investment is that when the price of the oil moves your percentage moves with it. Thus if you put up a margin of $10,000 (commodities always trade in dollars) that might be covering a contract worth $200,000. If the price moves 10%, your gain could be $20,000.

Good news, bad news

That's the good news. What's the bad news? First, apart from little nasties like market spreads, you have just as much chance of the price going down as up (assuming you're a buyer). Secondly, the rates of commission charged by the more unscrupulous brokers are ridiculous. They tell you it's never more than 5%, but what they mean is 5% of the value of the total contract, not 5% of your investment. It could be a very high percentage of your investment. Scrupulous brokers will charge

you under 1%. Thirdly, your money may get invested something like this.

You have given the broker $10,000 to invest for you in the commodity market, convinced that he can do it better than you can. He feels sugar is a good buy and buys 20 lots of $200. He's right, and the price moves up to $220. He sells, giving the profits from five of the lots to you and keeping the profits from the other 15 for himself. You, of course, are pleased and the broker, still bullish, suggests you buy another 20 lots at $220. This time he is wrong and the price moves down to $205. Guess who takes the total loss on the 20 lots?

Get in there, boy

There are stories, apocryphal I am sure, of certain firms taking the money, telling the clients which investments they are making – of course they turn out to be losers – and then just pocketing the money without speculating with it at all. It's a hype business, and the methods said to be used by some firms seem appalling. The salesmen are apparently not allowed to sit down while they are working, and are constantly harassed by the directors with encouraging remarks like 'Get in there, boy', or, if successful, 'Good close, man. Good close.'

A tape recorder is played loudly in the background to make it sound like a dealing room on the other end of the phone. Press headlines are used to encourage the punters to speculate – 'Platinum must move up sharply now, Mrs Wickens. Have you read in the paper this morning about another call for sanctions against South Africa?' Commission rates are such that to whip up enthusiasm on a slack day a director may put £2,000 in fivers on the table and offer it to the first person to do five trades. Motorbike messengers are sent to people's homes to pick up cheques. Get that money in, boy.

London Metal Exchange

The LME, which deals in hard commodities, i.e. copper, tin, lead and aluminium, has had its own Big Bang prompted by the collapse of the Tin Council, which owed brokers on the Exchange £500 million.

Before that the LME exhibited many of the worst aspects of the City – the long lunch, the large gin and tonics and the absence of any concern about future development. Brokers, grown fat on the easy profits of the 1970s, had become short-term greedy. Now perhaps they need to be long-term greedy. They will be helped by new regulations

HEAVY METAL

Open outcry: eager young tigers shout the odds at the Metal Exchange

Metal fatigue: Metal Exchange brokers under stress

brought in after the tin fiasco by the SIB, the Securities and Investments Board.

The old buffers on the board and committee of the Exchange have been augmented or in some cases replaced by more aggressive and thoughtful younger men, referred to as 'young tigers' in a management report produced by Price Waterhouse. Just in time, as with many other parts of the City, the LME is moving into the Thatcherite world of tough competition and efficient operation.

London Bullion Market

Meanwhile, not far away – in an oak-panelled room at the London office of merchant banker N.M. Rothschild, to be precise – that other hard commodity, gold, is being 'fixed'.

There are gold markets all round the world, probably a dozen or more from Chicago to Hong Kong, but they all look to the London gold fix. It is still the most important influence in international gold contracts. London is also important in the physical market. The 'actuals' come in daily on flights from Johannesburg and Moscow. It's insured at $1 an ounce – expensive (cement only costs $.02 an ounce in the first place, and never mind the insurance).

The big five bullion dealers – Rothschild, Samuel Montagu, Sharps Pixley, Mocatta & Goldsmid and the Australian Mase Westpac – 'fix' the price twice a day, at 10.30 a.m. and 3 p.m. (the price can change dramatically before 3 p.m. because of the economic data released from the USA between 1.30 and 2.30). The chairman, usually the Rothschild representative, announces an opening price. The others then report by telephone to their offices, who report back to them their clients' buying or selling requirements at the quoted price. If the buys and sells do not match, the procedure is repeated at a higher or lower price until equilibrium is reached.

Sellers would probably be the leading producers – South Africa, Canada, the USSR. Buyers could be industrial users, banks or speculators. In quiet times equilibrium can be reached quickly. In more volatile times, dealing can last for some time and become animated. When finally everyone is agreed that a balance has been reached, each representative lowers the Union Jack in front of him. When all five flags are down the price is fixed.

Mystical power

Gold has always held a mystical power. Indeed until the First World War all major Western currencies were backed by gold. The inflation and expenditure of that war killed the Gold Standard, and although Britain tried to restore it, we finally abandoned it in the financial crisis of 1931. The USA abandoned it in 1933, though it still pledged to redeem all dollars held by foreigners at $35 an ounce until 1971. Once that was abandoned, the price, artificially held back for decades, soared until it reached $800 an ounce during the Iranian crisis of 1980 before falling back to around $450 an ounce in 1988.

There is, in a sense, a dangerous situation because many nations' assets consisting of gold are virtually unsaleable in any quantity. Gold's price has been held so high that its practical uses are limited. But a collapse in the price is unlikely – too many people have a vested interest in keeping it up.

THE TWICE DAILY FIX

Silence is golden: a quiet day in Rothschild's gold price fixing room

STRESSFUL LIFFE

Plenty of work for the cleaners: the trading floor at LIFFE

Financial Futures Market

When the London International Financial Futures Exchange (LIFFE) opened in September 1982, thanks to the foresight and persistence of the City visionary John Barkshire, many of the pre-Big Bang brokers found these fellows just a little too uncouth. The trading floor of the Stock Exchange was then still peopled with gilts brokers in top hats, no women, and no one without a tie (anyone without one was debagged. Actually debagging often happened for no reason at all, just as there were no reasons for setting fire to people's *Daily Mail*s while they read them.) In complete contrast, the LIFFE traders at the Royal Exchange wear colourful blazers to mark them out when they are on the floor, and communicate through an incomprehensible tic-tac system. Their accents were scarcely believable to the traditional brokers back in 1982. Some, they saw with horror, wore mohican haircuts, many didn't wear ties, and one of them didn't even wear shoes. It was brash, it was noisy, there was money to be made and they didn't give a damn about anything else.

Don't miss a trade

Dealing in financial futures is a stressful job, with a typical broking room operating from 5.30 a.m., when it's plugged into Singapore, through to 9.30 p.m., by which time it's Chicago and New York. It operates on the old familiar open out-cry basis and clients can get upset if you just miss a trade when each contract is $1 million if it's short (i.e. three months) Eurodollars or £500,000 if it's short sterling. Tension builds

as each market opens, so that for example with short sterling opening at 8.15, everyone is a little twitchy from 8 a.m. onwards. In the more conventional operations commissions are not in the same league as some of the commodity brokers. In fact for institutions where firms like Goldman Sachs, Salomon Brothers and BZW are operating they are £12–13 per contract for a round trip, i.e. both buying and selling. But then the clients are institutions and are buying or selling a lot of contracts of $1 million or £500,000.

A desirable future

You can make a futures market in anything. We all know that property's a good thing to invest in these days, but best of all is property futures. Speculators have been buying expensive flats as yet unbuilt but due for completion in the 1990s. They only have to put down £50,000 on a flat that will cost £500,000 in 1991. What they hope is that the flat will increase at, say, 10% a year so that in a year's time it's worth, say, £550,000. No big deal except when you realize that the extra £50,000 is on an outlay of £50,000 and the profit is 100% not 10% – thank you very much. Of course, the property market could collapse as it did in 1973, and then you have committed yourself to paying £500,000 and the flat may only be saleable, if at all, at £300,000. Like trading at FOX and LIFFE, it is not for the faint-hearted.

Loud clothes and louder voices: LIFFE traders

-3- THE POWER HOUSES

THE OLD LADY

Banks

The Bank of England is in an anomalous situation. It was nationalized in 1946 and the then Labour Chancellor of the Exchequer, Stafford Cripps, used to refer to it as 'my creature'. It is of course the government's banker; but on the other hand it represents very private City interests in the corridors of Whitehall. One day it can be arguing for greater flexibility in regulations for the City, and the next it can be telling the chairman of Morgan Grenfell to fire Christopher Reeves and Graham Walsh because it has been instructed to by the Chancellor, Nigel Lawson.

The Johnson Matthey affair

Even when it was a private concern the Bank carried out many of the functions that it does today, one of the most notable of which is to minimize crises in other banks. Thus in the 1890 Baring crisis the Bank was able to organize other banks into a rescue fund. Again in the secondary banking crisis of 1973-4 the Bank arranged the famous Lifeboat to save the financial system from complete collapse. Its most recent salvage operation concerned Johnson Matthey, when over the weekend of 29-30 September 1984 nearly two hundred bankers were summoned to the deserted City to hammer out a rescue package before play began again on Monday morning. The saving of Johnson Matthey brought a great deal of criticism not only from the media (predictable) but also from other banks (perhaps not

so predictable). If some little-known bank was going to be rescued, where was the moral sanction on any lending institution to take care in its loan policies? The criticism increased when it was revealed that the Bank had been very slow to act on the obvious warning signals of impending disaster emanating from Johnson Matthey.

The Bank still sees itself as having a strong role to play in monetary policy as well as in the field of investor protection. The latter has become a more international problem as investors play the 24-hour markets.

Privatization? You must be joking. Like Sir Stafford Cripps, Thatcher wants it as her creature – she needs total control to help enforce her economic policies.

Solid as the Bank of England: Sir John Soane's statue on the building he designed

PECULIAR
POLICIES

The Big Four

Years ago the big high street or clearing banks – Lloyds, Barclays, National Westminster and the Midland – came to an arrangement whereby they did not compete for each other's customers and where they levied exactly the same charges. Employees joined them from school, were paid abysmally, and, provided they could stand it and didn't do anything silly like trying to lend money to budding entrepreneurs or anyone who actually needed some, they could expect to progress gently right through to retirement. Their main task was to make members of the public feel like naughty schoolboys if they wanted to borrow any money, and they certainly did not lend it to them unless the collateral was absolutely cast-iron. They were most emphatically not in the Risk Business. If on the other hand you could prove you had no need for the money, they fell over themselves in their eagerness to give it to you.

Lending to dodgy countries

However, for some peculiar reason these same pedagogues, as you will see, managed to lend huge sums – and I mean *billions* of pounds – to foreigners in dodgy countries thousands of miles away, who saw them coming, took the money and never paid them back. Actually, the bankers didn't mind the Argentines, Mexicans, Brazilians, Nigerians and so on not returning the capital as long as they didn't actually say they wouldn't, because then they could pretend they would and put the loan as an asset in their balance sheet. What bankers do *not* like is not being paid their interest.

SOUTH AMERICAN STITCH-UP

Then, as now, Banker He Spoke with Forked Tongue – what they actually thought was something along the lines of 'The British public will finance us through our other mistakes. They can borrow money from us at 3 or 4% over ridiculously high base rates, and they can also lend us money on which of course we won't pay any interest, and furthermore why don't we charge them for the privilege? And how about making them pay us a fixed fee every time they write out a cheque? Think they'll wear all that, ho ho? The haven't any option – of course they will!' Yes, we did, and we still do. No wonder Rowan Atkinson had bank managers alongside seal-killers in Hell in his one-man show!

I'm sorry, Mrs Roddick

'I'm sorry, Mrs Roddick. If you think this bank is lending you £5,000 to start a cosmetics shop then you're very much

mistaken. We're not here to help women start new businesses. If you're so keen on cosmetics why don't you apply for a job with Boots?'

'Senor Gonzalez, if you wish to make that 500 billion pesetas rather than 400 billion I'm sure that's fine with my people in London.'

Ten years later Anita Roddick's Body Shop is one of the darlings of the market, with franchised shops throughout the country and the beginnings of a world operation already in place. A local businessman loaned Anita what the banks would not, and when Body Shop was floated five years later the £5,000 was worth £13.5 million. In 1988 it is worth over £30 million.

The South American loan remains a loan. Keep it under your sombrero, but not a peseta of the principal has been repaid and there have been plenty of problems over the interest payments. The bank would have kept quiet about this, except that the American bank Citicorp decided to be honest about its loans to Central and South America and write them off. Others had to make provisions too.

In 1987 provisions for debts in developing countries were made as follows:

Lloyds	£1,066,000,000
Midland	£1,016,000,000
Barclays	£713,000,000
NatWest	£610,000,000
TOTAL	£3,405,000,000

In fact the situation is much worse than this. The provision is only about a third of the debt whereas, in view of the fact that Third World debt is traded in the City at an average of 25–30% of its face value, the provision should be more like 70–75%. The Bank of England put pressure on the banks not to make bigger provisions. If they did, those that owed the money would say:

Not mates with her bank manager: Anita Roddick with friend

'You've written off 70%, we'll only pay 30%.'

Even if the man in Shoreham-on-Sea had got it right and lent Mrs Roddick £5,000, the £30 million their stake would have been worth would not have helped much towards paying that lot off. No, unfortunately; what it needs to pay it off is you and me and Peter and all the other suckers up and down the country paying usurious interest rates and Olympian monthly charges.

City Banks

Surely all those bankers in the City with their posh accents and their big salaries are cleverer than this? Yes, they are, though in some cases they are still ruled by the people brought up to lend only if there is full collateral to cover the loan.

Previously in the City there were three types of bank: the clearing bank, the merchant bank and the overseas bank. They all kept to their own sphere of activity. Competition was extremely limited, particularly amongst the clearing banks who had long ago decided that competition was pointless particularly when, with both government and Bank of England approval, you could also use, free of charge, all the money the plebs kept in their current accounts. The merchant banks too did not compete too strongly. Each had his clients. New ones came along from time to time, but one did not poach.

Crossing the Chinese Walls

Big Bang changed all that. Henceforth banks could own stockbrokers and jobbers, and foreigners could operate on the Stock Exchange. Now the big guys were the investment banks: the British ones squared up to the American ones, and both looked over their shoulder at the Japanese. As in all good battles there were some effective light cavalry brigades around, in this case Swiss, German, French and Anzac. Brokers and jobbers were absorbed and the banks offered all things to all men. They could act as a company's banker, raise long-term debt or equity finance, make a market (buy and sell) in the securities involved, sell them to investors through their broking arm and buy them for the funds they managed. Get it right and you have a very big business making a lot of money. Get it wrong and you could be tempted to cross the Chinese Walls that are now supposed to exist in every financial conglomerate.

> **CHINESE WALLS** Invisible barriers in internal communication between different areas of the new financial conglomerates. They are necessary because one area of a conglomerate may be selling a company's shares while another area is plotting that company's takeover.

ALL IN
BED
TOGETHER

THE CITY SLICKER'S LEAGUE TABLE

Following the acquisitions and mergers, before and after Big Bang, where did all the old firms go, and which division – and, perhaps more importantly, at which end of the division – has everyone finished up in 1988?

DIVISION ONE

	WHO	OWNER NOW	PUGH'S VIEW
Champions	Mullens Rowe & Pitman Akroyd & Smithers	S. G. Warburg	Always been good long-term planners. Think things through. If you are lucky enough to be offered a job by them, take it.
2.	de Zoete & Bevan Wedd Durlacher Mordaunt	Barclays	Now called BZW. Lots of muscle and will succeed, but plenty of drama en route with people coming and going for £1 million plus.
3.	Cazenove	Stayed aloof	Good connections and legendary placing power. Even the Guinness scandal has only dropped them to third position.
4.	Grieveson Grant	Kleinwort Benson	Well run and with the government's ear on privatizations.
5.	James Capel	Hongkong and Shanghai Bank	Clinically efficient with best team of equity analysts.
6.	Smith Bros Scott Goff Layton	N. M. Rothschild	High-pedigree operation.
7.	Samuel Montagu	Midland	Samuel Montagu put together some very successful financial packages, though they want to watch their parent after what it did to Greenwell & Co.
8.	Lazards	Stayed aloof (though of course controlled by Pearson Group)	Good investment advice. Like Kleinworts, well in with HMG. Not done too much underwriting.
9.	Charterhouse Tilney	Royal Bank of Scotland	Third Division for years until Victor Blank took them up on the back of dramatic Woolworth victory.
10.	Phillips & Drew Edwards, Jones & Wilcox Moulsdale	Union Bank of Switzerland	Used to be efficient if rather grey. P & D thought to be the strength, but after failures in placing Blue Arrow and Robinson on the verge of being relegated.

DIVISION TWO

	WHO	OWNER NOW	PUGH'S VIEW
1.	Pember & Boyle Pinchin Denny	Morgan Grenfell	MG would be well up in Division One but were automatically relegated for their close involvement in the Guinness scandal.
2.	Panmure Gordon	North Carolina National Bank	Subtle choice of owner. Retained partner incentive with capital backing.
3.	Alexanders Laing & Cruikshank	Crédit Lyonnais	This is where Tony Parnes was a half commission man.
4.	Capel-Cure Myers	Australia & NZ Banking Group	Solid Second Division player with good advice to small companies, knowledge of USM and large private client list.
5.	Fielding Newson-Smith Bisgood Bishop Wood Mackenzie	County NatWest	WoodMac were well run, but made a bad marriage with Hill Samuel who, in turn, went to TSB. County NatWest have enjoyed, if that is the word, some well-publicized traumas.
6.	Schroders	Stayed aloof	On their way back to Division One.
7.	Morgan Stanley	Stayed aloof	Blue chip on way to Division One. Need to resist temptation to fire some excellent new recruits.
8.	Barings	Stayed aloof	Good away form, especially in Japan.
9.	Robert Fleming	Stayed aloof	Slithering – nearly turned themselves into an engineering company with merchant banking connections in spring 1988.
10.	Hoare Govett Charles Pulley	Security Pacific	At school you fail exams if you can't count, in the City you lose clients and therefore get relegated.

DIVISION THREE

	WHO	OWNER NOW	PUGH'S VIEW
1.	Buckmaster & Moore	Crédit Suisse First Boston	Drifting down. Not helped by high-profile transfers at US headquarters.
2.	Simon & Coates Laurie Milbank	Chase Manhattan	Megabucks were paid for the acquisitions, but not much megathought went into the assimilation.
3.	Henderson Crosthwaite Beardsley Bishop	Guinness Peat	Lots of problems in parent company.
4.	Strauss Turnbull	Hambros	It is sad to find these at the bottom of Division Three, but then it was sad to find Wolverhampton Wanderers in Division Four.
5.	Messel	Shearson Lehman	
6.	Hill Samuel	TSB	
7.	J. A. Scrimgeour Vickers da Costa	Citicorp	

SERIOUS FEES

At Lazards, the merchant bank that stayed aloof in Big Bang, they felt it was mad to buy teams of brokers and jobbers and pay huge sums not only for the people but also for the names, even if the names had been around for a hundred years. Greenwells had been around since the nineteenth century. By early 1988 Midland had managed to close down its entire equity operation. Messels had been around since the eighteenth century and was the Queen's broker – hands up who knows where it is now? Lazards' view was: 'Let's hire the good guys but not their fancy names.' They didn't buy a stockbroker; they don't make markets. They expect to survive by offering independent and creative advice.

Corporate Finance

The real excitement in the merchant banking arena is in the corporate finance department. That department comes alive, at least as far as the outside world is concerned, when it is involved in a takeover, especially a contested one, and earns serious fees – typically £1 million plus on a £200 million deal.

But perhaps more significant than the fees a merchant bank will charge in a takeover battle is the commission it will take for underwriting the issue of new shares to finance the bids. Many say that London is now the world's most efficient market for raising equity capital at short notice.

For an underwriting fee of 2% a bank will agree to guarantee the issue of large lines of new shares. Out of this fee it will typically pay a broker $\frac{1}{4}\%$ to arrange the distribution and a fee of $1\frac{1}{4}\%$, or maybe 1%, to other institutional investors to participate in the sub-underwriting. Thus the bank organizing the deal retains $\frac{1}{2}\%$ – nice when it works and all goes smoothly.

Occasionally it does not and the bank can lose heavily, as Robert Fleming found to its cost in early 1988 when it misjudged its broker's ability (the broker was Phillips & Drew) to lay off the underwriting of Robinson's bid for Crowther and could have got landed with £125 million of Robinson stock. Similarly many of the banks underwriting the BP issue in October 1987 quickly clocked up multi-million pound losses, wiping out in one week perhaps a year's commission earned on other deals.

Mistakes occur occasionally, but they are outweighed by the successes, such as the underwriting of $560 million of equity and debt by Samuel Montagu for little WPP when it bought the once mighty JWT against the competition of other US buyers

who only got the guarantee from US banks of using their 'best efforts' to raise the finance.

Most merchant banks now feel it is important to have other capital behind them – Samuel Montagu has Midland, Charterhouse has the Royal Bank of Scotland, County has NatWest, Hill Samuel has TSB. Others feel there is a niche for the relatively small specialist adviser.

Certainly the aggression shown by some has been remarkable. Morgan Grenfell, staid and stuffy in the sixties, became ultra-aggressive in the early eighties. Any company chairman embarking on a bid felt almost obliged to use them. The corporate finance department was paid by results and they went all out to get them. As a result the authorities complained, and in the end it all boiled over into arrests and dismissals.

Merchant banks are all about the people who run them, and reputations can rise and sink fast. With their higher-risk strategies and innovative financing technique the gap between the dozen or so key corporate finance executives in the City and the remainder has widened dramatically.

Takeovers need real money

A major impact of the Crash on the corporate finance side has been the way takeovers are being financed. At the end of the long bull market the high-flying companies with share prices to match could use their own paper, their own shares, to fund the takeovers. They could do this because d'Arcy would have no difficulty in persuading the institutions to take more shares, confident that they would soon be rising again. Come the Crash, and a possible bear market, and nobody wants any more shares, thank you very much, 'especially as the last lot we took are now at a considerable

D'ARCY – THE CORPORATE FINANCIER

D'Arcy went to Harrow and Oxford and is pretty clued up but he is not, in terms of sharpness or financial creativity, in the same league as insider dealer Gerard whom you'll meet later. He is involved in corporate finance deals – mostly takeovers – because of his smoothness, political acumen and wide range of social contacts. The law does not trust Gerard. You should not trust d'Arcy. He talks to most people as though there is an insufferably bad smell under his nose. He does what he is told to do by his superiors whether he thinks it is right or not. The only judgement he makes is whether it will advance his career. He is very unpleasant to work with, even worse to work for, horrible to meet, grovelling and sycophantic to his superiors, to people with titles, and to anyone he feels may be of use to him. He would probably vote for Hitler if he appeared on the Surrey hustings.

WHIZZ-KIDS AND BIG DEALS

discount'. Takeovers are now for real money, either actual pounds sterling or for pounds sterling lent by a bank.

If no one hanged for pouring billions into Brazilian and Mexican pockets, one or two did for some of the relatively small but well-publicized losses of the new investment arms of the big conglomerates. In early 1988 two of County NatWest's stars felt the trapdoor drop under their feet. The chairman, Charles Villiers, and the chief executive, Jonathan Cohen, made the Supreme Sacrifice.

The clanger of the year

In the macho world of '87 with City whizz-kids all over the front pages and the colour supplements, never mind the business pages, big deals were the name of the game. County NatWest Securities, trying to keep up in this world, thought they had pulled the deal of the year when they master-minded the biggest ever rights issue in London for Tony Berry's Blue Arrow Group, which bought the giant American employment company Manpower. Unfortunately they had bitten off more than they could chew and, despite all their pushing to place the stock, they had to take nearly 10% themselves, 4.9% in their fund management arm and 4.6% in the market-making arm. Several people including the Bank of England were not too happy about this. One is not supposed to have more than 5% of a company's shares without declaring it openly. The deal of the year turned into the clanger of the year as the Crash came and Blue Arrow's shares fell by 50%. Loss – £47 million. Not to be compared with the cost of skyscrapers in Rio, but still loadsa money.

Sunday Times,
21 February 1988

County's reputation hits rock bottom

by Judi Bevan, Deputy City Editor

THE chapter of disasters that has hit County NatWest, the investment bank owned by National Westminster, has sent the City's perception of the bank plummeting.

As one of the four clearing-bank formations of Big Bang financial players, it is heading for the wooden-spoon award in almost every area, and the futures of Jonathan Cohen, the chief executive, and of Charles Villiers, the chairman, are in doubt.

The full extent of the financial damage sustained after the crash in world markets in October should become clear on Tuesday, when National Westminster announces full-year profits for 1987. Friday's report in The Economist that the Department of

Cohen: admitting to errors

"golden handcuffs" but even so only half of those who joined are still there now. Some left recently in the spate of redundancies. Others left with great acrimony — for example, Charles Peel, head of Fielding's sales team, who could not stand the bureaucracy of being part of a clearing bank. "Charlie never went to management committee meetings so in the end Cohen booted him off," remarks one observer.

Cohen was so annoyed by Peel's decision to join Morgan Grenfell Securities that he insisted on sticking to the details of the contract which barred Peel from working in the London market for a year.

Publicly Cohen was sanguine. "We are global players

Pawnbroking

There is an alternative to borrowing money from a bank. Rupert Galliers-Pratt went to Eton and lives in Belgravia. He works in the Walworth Road and he runs Britain's most successful pawnbroking operation, Harvey & Thompson. In case you thought pawnbrokers were hole-in-the-wall operations run by miserly recluses, Harvey & Thompson has 20 branches, makes a million profit and is a PLC on the Unlisted Securities Market (USM). And although the head office is dahn Wolworf Road, some of the branches are in distinctly up-market or up-and-coming areas such as Clapham, Fulham, Golders Green and King Street, Manchester, where they rub shoulders with Jaeger, Next and Laura Ashley.

No down-and-outs

The clients are not down-and-outs but the small businessman who needs money in a hurry and cannot wait for his local bank to make up its mind, or a Slicker who wants to stag a new issue, or someone who wants to raise real money against the jewellery granny left her. What ordinary bank will lend money against jewellery?

Loans are for six months and can be repaid any time without penalty. The interest must be paid within the six months. If the interest is not paid, after a further four months the jewellery will be sold at public auction; once the loan and interest have been deducted, the rest will be returned. If the interest is paid, the loan can be renewed – revolving credit. Smashing.

So is the rate of interest – 4% a month, but it is not compounded so it amounts to 48% a year, plus a £20 facility fee for each loan. It is higher than the banks, just a bit,

and the credit card companies, but if you need the money . . . .

Take along your Rolex

The next drawback is – what is pawnable? Not your 1953 Lesney Matchbox Coronation Coach, nor your Crombie overcoat. H&T are only interested in jewellery, watches, gold, silver and precious stones. If Darren, our half commission man from Essex, ever falls on hard times – which is difficult to imagine – he will be all right with his gold Rolex Oyster because it is difficult to fake. Corporate financier d'Arcy may have more trouble with his Cartier – 'It's brilliantly made, guv, but we're only interested in the gold content, so we'll lend you 50% of the meltdown value.' D'Arcy shudders delicately at the mention of the word Meltdown, and departs unfulfilled.

THE CARTIER MELTDOWN

PENSION POWER

Institutions

Every day we read that the institutions are back in the market, or that they are on the sidelines, or that they are shunning an issue, or that they are fully invested, or that they will not easily forgive Sir Ralph Halpern for his greedy share option scheme.

What are these mighty institutions, and why are they so important? In 1939 private individuals owned 80% of the ordinary share capital of the public companies in this country. By the early 1980s this had dropped to 30%. Individuals had been replaced by the institutions – mainly life assurance companies and pension funds but also investment trusts, unit trusts and banks. When Thatcher came to power in 1979 about 5% of the adult population owned shares. After all the hype of privatization that has now increased to probably 12%, but the institutions are still completely dominant in the markets.

Staggering growth rate

As the provision for pensions grew, some of the pension funds of large organizations grew at a staggering rate. The Post Office and the National Coal Board have funds measured in billions, and large companies that perform badly and whose shares are given a low rating can find their companies valued at less than the worth of their own pension funds' investments.

Major stock market investment decisions are in the hands of remarkably few people – the fund managers. Approximately 50–60 of them are the 'shareholders' of our British public companies and can have profound effects on the jobs of others.

Imagine, for example, that an institution owns a significant slice of a company being bid for, say 1%, as did one of the BZW-managed funds of Birmid Qualcast when it was bid for by cement giant Blue Circle in the winter of 1987-8. David Acland, the chairman of the BZW fund involved, had been a director of Blue Circle for many years before leaving some months earlier amidst rumours of a palace revolution. As the deadline drew near it was clear that the result would be close and it became crucially important which side every institution supported.

Getting your sums wrong

With five days to go Dick Withers Green at BZW told the press that he was accepting the Blue Circle bid. Blue Circle therefore relaxed about that holding and concentrated on persuading those who were still uncommitted. At the last minute, to the surprise and consternation of Blue Circle, BZW changed their mind and their 1% stayed with Birmid. It was crucial: Blue Circle, having been told by their broker Hoare Govett they had won by 9,000 shares – 0.0001% of the total shareholding – discovered that Hoare Govett couldn't count too well and that they had in fact lost by about 400,000 shares; still, much less than the BZW holding.

For years the fund manager was regarded as a plodder and was paid a plodder's wage, but in the new City his performance is being checked quarterly and he can no longer hide behind the dictum 'Judge me on a 25-year basis.' The pressure to perform has increased, but luckily for him so has the pay. Furthermore that much loved performance-related bonus has also spread to his office. Thus talented performers can be expected to earn around £100,000 plus bonuses, and in total are paid £500 million.

You will be surprised to learn that, on average, the performance of these highly paid fund managers does not match that of the indexes (FT30, Footsie etc.). The reason is that the institutions comprise such a major part of the market that in effect they *are* the market. Therefore their average performance is bound to be close to that of the indexes, but the fund managers have to bear the dealing costs and spreads when buying and selling, which the indexes don't.

Why, therefore, employ fund managers? Why not just buy the indexes? You *can* invest in funds which do just that, and, of course, although the average performance is below that of the indexes, there are certain fund managers who outperform them, sometimes quite comfortably. Investors who use fund managers are clearly hoping to find one of those. If so, they will need to change their fund manager frequently as this year's winner is quite likely to be next year's loser.

Short-term profit

Short-termism is a phrase you hear very frequently, especially from the defending side in a takeover bid. It means that institutions are selling their shares to a predator because it will improve their short-term performance. In our Blue Circle v. Birmid bid, Bob Armstrong, an institutional fund manager at Robert Fleming responsible for handling funds of £700 million, was faced with the dilemma of whether he should accept 380p for his 500,000 shares. He had, after all, bought them at 80p and would therefore show a profit of £1.5 million. If the bid failed the price would probably fall back to £3 and he would lose £400,000. Support the existing management who had done well, as everyone agreed, or take the money? He took the money.

Another small company which felt itself betrayed by the institutions was the Yorkshire supermarket group Hillards. After

they had lost their battle for independence to Tesco in 1987, the chairman, Peter Hartley, let fly at the investment chief of the biggest investment institution of all, the Prudential. He said, 'This is another example of the selfish and irresponsible attitude adopted by City financiers who put money before jobs.' As if to help him make his point Tesco quickly started firing Hillards' employees. But then, that's presumably why the Pru backed them – these family businesses are too 'paternal', a City euphemism for employing too many people.

Birmid's chief executive thanks his lucky stars he wasn't mown down by the fund managers

GULP DOWN THE GUINNESS

The Guinness story is littered with dodgy dealings

Fund managers also have to contend with their trustees as well as with irate chairmen of companies in which they have invested. The trustees are ultimately the group responsible to those who have invested the money for the managers to manage, but of course they have a tendency to indulge their own whims before they think of these investors. One disagreement finished in the High Court in 1984 when the five trustees from the National Union of Mineworkers – you will remember that 1984 was their *annus mirabilis* when everyone in the world was wrong except them – told the investment manager of the British Coal pension fund, David Prosser, that he was not to invest in South Africa or in competing energy sources. The court ruled that investment decisions should be based on investment criteria and not personal prejudice.

Not covered in glory

Apart from their actions during the Guinness bid for Distillers the institutions based in the City, as opposed to those based in Edinburgh, did not cover themselves in glory in what became known as the Thomas Risk Affair. Ernest Saunders, the chief executive of Guinness, had promised to make Sir Thomas Risk, Governor of the Bank of Scotland, chairman of the combined group if Guinness were successful in its bid for Distillers. Apart from their own share price, for which several formerly illustrious – illustrious in their own eyes, anyway – operators could end up in jail, the other key factor in Guinness's successful takeover of Distillers was this promise to install a Scottish chairman. After the bid was won, Saunders cynically reneged on his promise.

The DTI comes a-knockin'

Egged on by the journalists who supported his cause, the institutions supported Saunders at the extraordinary general meeting called to appoint the new Guinness board. One colourful representative of the institutions stood out against him – Graeme Knox, chief investment manager of the Scottish Amicable. But as he was a red-bearded Scot who looked like a warring clansman, everyone was able to say, 'Well, he would, wouldn't he?' It was not a good day for the institutions. It was suggested that Saunders had already broken his word and should not be trusted. The institutions refused to listen and voted by 322 million to 27 million for Saunders. Three months later the DTI came a-knock knock knockin' on Saunders' door.

Edinburgh

Where does Edinburgh fit into the New City? We keep hearing about the mafia around Charlotte Square, but how do they fit in? It is the only other significant base for financial institutions in the UK.

The answer is they don't fit in because they don't want to. It was always the main thrust of their marketing of themselves as financial advisers and managers of your money that they were away from the hurly-burly and frenetic, sheep-like behaviour of those smart alecs in London. As a result of this Edinburgh is quietly successful, but must be worrying about a future where very big or very small is deemed to be beautiful – but not in between.

Irritatingly from the Scottish point of view, England – and specifically the City – is where the real action is. Look at Guinness and Distillers. It was going to have a Scottish chairman and a Scottish head office, and the new board were going to live in Scotland. Wrong. Look at Britoil. Presumably it was set up in Glasgow for some reason. Presumably the government retained a Golden Share for some reason. If so, the reasons were ignored when BP took them out.

Sober suits on the shuttle

One of the self-imposed handicaps which has held back the Scots in competing on

equal terms with the City is their reluctance to stop warring with each other like their clannish ancestors. It has appeared at times that the fund managers round Charlotte Square would rather see funds go to London than to others in the Square. Nevertheless there is still big money around Charlotte Square and some big holders of stock. Ambitious company chairmen and their PR advisers cannot afford to ignore them, or do so at their peril. The shuttle is always full of sober-suited gentlemen winging to and from the City in the North.

THE CHARLOTTE SQUARE MAFIA

GOLDEN SHARE A share retained, usually but not necessarily, by the government, giving the holder ultimate control of a company, sometimes indefinitely and sometimes for a limited and specified period of time.

NEW YORK'S SLICE OF THE ACTION

Foreign Influence

The Americans Chase Manhattan bought Laurie Milbank and Simon & Coates, at Security Pacific they bought Hoare Govett, at Citicorp they bought Scrimgeour Vickers, at Credit Suisse First Boston (Americans with a flash name) they bought Buckmaster & Moore, at North Carolina National Bank they bought Panmure Gordon – and the Royal Bank of Canada bought Kitcat & Aitken. Pause for breath.

Just as they brought American customs to British business 20 years ago, so the Americans introduced some new techniques to the City. The first was good – high pay levels; the second was not so good – longer hours; the third was worse – rationalization.

And it was not only the ones which bought British houses that were here. Leading investment houses stepped up their presence – Bache Securities, Goldman Sachs, Merrill Lynch (the largest US securities house), Salomon Brothers and Shearson

Salomon's dealing warehouse at Victoria Plaza

Lehman. Big in the world's biggest market, these Americans are going to make sure the City never slips back to its old ways.

Hyping the team

In terms of recruiting the best the Americans made a lot of noise and offered loadsa money. However, they were not always successful because their reputation for hire and fire made many people turn them down.

The American corporate financier plugs into his offices round the States to sell British ADRs. Shearson, known as a wire house because it has wires all over the States, was all geared up to sell the BP issue through its six thousand retail offices across the country. That meant not only a big hit to the salesmen in New York, but tapes to all the regional sales managers throughout the States so that they could hype their own teams. Too bad that the Crash intervened and the parent company, Shearson Lehman, was left with $400 million worth of stock.

ADRs American depository receipts. As US citizens cannot buy foreign shares direct, ADRs are certificates issued by a bank showing that a specific number of a company's shares have been deposited with it. They are priced in US dollars and traded like any other American security.

But, undeterred, an American corporate financier can offer a very valuable commodity: in-depth knowledge of the US market. That is important, as any self-respecting, acquisition-minded business must at some stage look at the world's biggest market. Even the Brits, whether they be NatWest, Barclays, Lloyds, Midland, Mercury Securities or Kleinwort Grieveson, are going to struggle to compete in global terms with the likes of the Shearson Lehman Hutton combine. Shearson's retail sales force, Hutton's direct-sell sales force and Lehman's institutional sales force work in a country of 230 million people, 25% of whom are active investors.

Eat and deal, deal and eat

Nothing exemplifies the worship of Mammon quite like the dealing room at Salomon Brothers. The dealing room in New York is big and busy and impresses clients – they *look* as though they're makin' dough, though they might not be, in fact. Salomon wanted to create the same atmosphere in the City of London. It could not be done in the old City buildings, so they moved out to Victoria Plaza where they could have their big dealing room and potential clients could look down on it from the executive offices above. With so much dealing, any time out, whether to the loo or for lunch, costs money and is resented. A thousand people work in the building, but there are only 120 seats in the cafeteria. Lunch boxes are provided so that you can eat and deal, deal and eat. We've gotta be ready for the Street at 1.30, man. Round the dealing room with its three hundred dealers and of course its three hundred screens is the electronic scoreboard, with the latest prices and deals constantly revolving. And, American style, they are all there, from senior trader to junior.

£2.5 million in Japan

The American corporate financier came to the City and threw his weight around ostentatiously. His Japanese counterpart did the same, but with much more circumspection. As salaries and perks were being bid up in the Big Bang revolution, the Japanese found it difficult to recruit. Why work for the Japanese when the Americans will pay you more? Post-Crash it's different. The

A yen to make a mark: a Tokyo money dealer starts his day

Americans are a bit unreliable, the Brits have certainly cut back on the salaries and perks, the Japanese seem to be long-term players and, boy oh boy, do *they* have a strong economy and financial muscle – Tokyo had to overtake New York as the biggest stock market in the world at some stage, but in all the brouhaha few noticed that it did so in one easy stride during the Crash. Nine months later the daily transactions were more than New York and London combined. Tokyo is also where Christopher Heath makes so much money for Barings that they can afford to pay him his £2.5 million salary and bonus.

The Tokyo market itself is highly speculative, and companies are rated on apparently ridiculous PE ratios in the fifties and sixties, sometimes even over a hundred. Because of this outsiders thought Tokyo must be the trigger for the end of the bull market. It was not, and the Japanese are marching through London setting up Nomura and Daiwa to be big players in the 1990s.

THE RISK BUSINESS

Lloyd's

Savanita, Sasse, Goldfinger Posgate, Peter Dixon and Cameron Webb, Kenneth Grob – lurching from one scandal to the next, the last ten years at Lloyd's seems to have been one long saga of scandal.

What is Lloyd's and how does it work? The simple answer is that at the time of writing it doesn't very well. Not happily, anyhow, and the reason is that the Lloyd's underwriters are less than pleased with the fabulous award-winning Richard Rogers-designed casing in which they try to work.

Packaging problems aside, Lloyd's is just another market. Just as the Stock Exchange is a market for buying and selling financial securities, so Lloyd's is a market for buying and selling risk. Get it right and you can make a fortune; get it wrong and you can lose your shirt. But with all the pomp and aura of tradition at Lloyd's, don't forget that what is called a Lloyd's Name does not have

Spreading the risk at Lloyd's

to be there to make the money. The nasty thing is that nor does he have to be there for someone to lose it for him. For over a hundred years professional underwriters have been able to insure risks not just for themselves but for non-working members, known as Names. As these underwriters can cause these non-working members to lose everything they possess, what can possibly be the attraction of being a Name?

What's in a Name?

To be a Name, you have to be able to show £100,000 of unencumbered assets excluding your principal residence. Further, you have to put up a reasonably substantial sum to be placed into a deposit fund held by Lloyd's, and this allows you to accept premium income in the insurance offered by the syndicate in which you participate.

This premium income is a multiple of the sum deposited. Two profits can then be enjoyed: the balance of the premium income over any claims, i.e. the normal underwriting profit, and the profit derived from the investment of premiums held by the syndicates. Furthermore, you still earn interest or dividends on your original capital. But the good news does not end there. The premiums can be invested to produce capital gains rather than income. Until the 1988 Budget capital gains, taxed at 30%, were a much better bet than income, which at the highest rates was taxed much higher. Losses can be offset against taxable income. And in years of high inflation there is even more good news. Lloyd's runs a three-year accounting system, effectively giving Names a three-year tax holiday. A tax bill of £15,000 in 1980 was effectively £10,000 by 1983, because of inflation.

There endeth the good news. Here is the bad. The huge influx of Names attracted by these advantages – membership grew from

6,000 in 1970 to over 30,000 in 1987 – did not really know what was going on, and some of them were taken for the most enormous ride, in some cases right into Carey Street. Anyway, capital gains are now taxed at 40%, the same as the highest rate of income tax. There were various scandals in the late seventies and early eighties, but in 1985 it was revealed that one of the most respected syndicates, PCW, run by Peter Cameron Webb, had helped itself to £40 million of the syndicate's money. You could scarcely get a purer fraud than that, but thanks to some bad underwriting there were also genuine losses of over £340 million – that's a lot of shirts.

Baby syndicates

Worse was to come. Investigations revealed that Cameron Webb had run 'baby syndicates' – syndicates which enjoyed the lushest business – and the easy profits from these were kept to themselves and their friends. Even worse was to come. Further investigation showed that this 'baby syndicate' ruse was not confined to the crooks but was commonly used by highly

respected underwriters, even member of the Lloyd's Council.

Put bluntly, it meant that you as a Name were not going to get the same deal as the underwriting agent who you thought was acting on your behalf, and whose interests were theoretically identical to yours. 'Baby syndicates' have now been banned, but not 'parallel syndicates'. Parallel means bigger baby.

A dead satellite gets collected

Lloyd's do not take their losses lightly. When the Lutine Bell rings to signal the loss of a ship – which it does quite frequently now, with the Gulf War and other local conflicts – there is always going to be a bad moment for a Name or two. When a claim is met in full, title in the property claimed passes to the syndicate(s), so in order to recoup as much of the loss as possible, salvage efforts are not inconsiderable. When an impressively expensive communications satellite packed up after only a few weeks in orbit, a syndicate booked time on the space shuttle to go and collect it.

WHEN THE BELL TOLLS

Working under pressure in the Lloyd's building

-4- *SERIOUS MONEY*

Flotations

In a bull market investors have to be dumb not to make money, but the serious money is made in takeovers and in public flotations of companies new to the stock market. For the owners of the companies it can mean very serious money indeed. Alan Sugar floated his company, Amstrad, in the early eighties. He retained over 50%, and as the company's capitalization approached £1 billion in 1987 his personal stake was worth half a billion – not bad for someone who started selling car aerials down the Old Kent Road about 15 years ago. How does he do it? According to

Branson makes a splash, Virgin takes a tumble

Sugar himself, just by giving the customer what he wants.

The knack for the sponsor, usually a merchant bank, who is promoting the issue is to pitch the shares at a price which will satisfy the owners but will allow prospective investors to feel they are getting a bargain. The government had no problems because the only owners they had to satisfy were the poor bloody taxpayers, and they didn't bother to consult them. They were therefore able to underprice their issues with impunity, thus ensuring a first-day premium. Others do not find it so easy and there have been many cases of severely overpriced issues, most notably American oil exploration stocks.

Virgin's nervous investors

Even Richard Branson's Virgin Group, which was growing strongly and enjoyed a considerable public following, opened at a discount. The institutions, as important in this field as every other, were not sure they liked the chairman of the company flying across the Atlantic in a balloon full of hot air and nearly killing himself, especially as they could not think of anyone else who worked at Virgin. That's the trouble with promoting your company through your own personality. You step off the pavement looking left, there's a bus coming from the right, and your share price goes through the floor. What price Amstrad without Sugar?

The city is a market-place

The City is a market-place and you should never forget it. At the end of the day

the same rules apply as they do in Petticoat Lane. Will people buy what you are trying to sell?

In the case of new issues they will if they can see a profit, but they are sensitive about buying something new and the slightest thing can turn a potential success into a bomb. The biggest recent example was the BP issue, where the slight thing was the October Crash. But there can be other factors.

No secrets

When shares are offered to the public the sponsor must produce a prospectus which has to contain all types of financial information about the company. It also gives some details about the directors. It is not mandatory to record every misdemeanour unless it is a factor likely to affect the running of the business. For example if the finance director had been convicted of fraud only 12 months earlier that might be considered a cause for concern.

The advice from the lawyers is always the same – if there are any skeletons, open the closet door and declare them in the prospectus. It may be cause for a few snide comments, but nothing more. Don't declare them, let some friendly competitor slip it to *Private Eye*, and it could be a big and damaging story.

A complete disaster

The flotation of the stamp auctioneers Stanley Gibbons was a complete disaster when it was discovered in the time between the flotation and the day dealings started that the managing director, Mr Clive Feigenbaum, had previously fallen foul of the philatelic authorities. Dealing in the shares had actually commenced, because the jobbers and brokers failed to notice that the Stock Exchange had not posted a Rule 195 notice, giving permission for dealings to begin. These dealings had to be unscrambled and ultimately the issue was withdrawn.

We are making you an offer you cannot refuse

SOCKS AND SHARES

The possibility of this kind of situation means that companies have almost gone to the other extreme in their paranoia. One company went public in early 1988 and there in the prospectus were details of the managing director having been convicted of assault and stealing golf clubs 30 years before.

Everyone laughed at the idea

In 1983 Sophie Mirman, who started work in the typing pool at Marks & Spencer, and her partner Richard Ross were willing to sell 49% of their business for £40,000. 'Everyone laughed at the idea. Investors, manufacturers, even landlords all thought Sock Shop was a silly name for a business and that the idea of a shop selling nothing but socks and tights was ridiculous.' Yet when the company was floated four years later the 49% was worth £31 million within half an hour of dealings starting. Silly idea it may have been. In fact it was stunningly simple. Socks were unglamorous

and treated as such by department stores, who never seemed to stock the right colour or size. Sock Shops were set up to offer well-designed, brightly coloured socks, stockings and tights.

No one wanted 49% – shame on you, Ronald Cohen and all your bevy of smooth venture capitalists – and in the end Barclays suggested a Government Small Firms Loan Guarantee Scheme (it must be this scheme's most conspicuous success). The first shop opened in Knightsbridge underground station in April 1983. Initially Sophie and Richard did everything themselves from cleaning the shop early in the morning to Mirman cycling off to collect the merchandise. They both served in the shop during the day and checked the stock at night. Within six months they opened another shop at Victoria.

Million-pound kiosks

Thereafter they expanded rapidly, and the company was floated with much hype at the peak of the bull market in early summer 1987. The offer was 53 times oversubscribed. There were 76,500 applications for 206 million shares, as opposed to the 3.9 million on offer. The allotment proved how pointless it was to stag even such a wild success. First of all there was a ballot, and then anyone who had applied for, say, 10,000 would receive only 200.

Against an offer price of 125p the shares opened at 205p and in frenetic trading rose to 290 before closing at 257p. At that price the 49% which no one had been interested in four years earlier was worth nearly £28 million. Someone noticed that, with the company capitalized at £56.5 million, each of Sock Shop's 43 little kiosks, most of them in the wind tunnels of our insalubrious main line stations, was valued at £1.3 million. Lord Sieff had known what he was doing

Sophie Mirman gets a foot in the door

when he advised his employee to do her own thing. He was also wise enough to become a non-executive director and a shareholder. And Sophie has been named 1988 Businesswoman of the Year.

High Tech, High Fashion

The stock market is a market and all the players in it merely traders. Don't forget, either, that it's also a fashion market. Sock Shop was the rage of '87 because it was a retailer which had found a niche in the market.

The rages of '82 and '83 were high-tech companies. On the crest of that wave two Cambridge boffins, Herman Hauser and Chris Curry, floated their company, Acorn Computers. They may have been a couple of hicks from the sticks, but in view of the current fashion the blue bloods Lazards sponsored the flotation and the exclusive Cazenove pushed the shares around. Initially Lazards were grateful – the shares rose smartly to 193p, valuing Hauser's and Curry's stakes in this one-product company at £103 million and £85 million: serious money. This was in March 1984. By 6 February 1985 they were suspended at 28p, having fallen to 22p earlier in the week. Lazards were fired by the company. Cazenove gratefully accepted this as an excuse to resign.

It was a stunning disaster. At Christmas 1983 Acorn BBC computers were like gold. At Christmas 1984 they were being discounted. For the Lazards and Cazenoves it was yesterday's fashion. Let's get on to the next one. The next one just happened to be the whisky business, but that's another story.

Wire and Plastic Products Ltd sounds really trendy, doesn't it? But adopt the eighties' fashion for initials and call it WPP, add a lot of Sorrell and a pinch of the rare spice Rabl, and you have a wonder stock which went from 30p to 1,000p in eighteen months. The 1,000p share price meant that WPP enjoyed a PE rating in the seventies, which means that the market was valuing its shares (its paper, to use the market jargon) at a massive 70 times its year's earnings. When you think that the PE ratings of ICI and Hanson Trust hover around the low teens, you can see that the market was expecting real fireworks from WPP.

When the party's over

In all bull markets you find companies like WPP, and as long as the bull market lasts their growth becomes self-fulfilling. If you can get your paper valued highly you can use it to buy the profits of less highly rated companies, or in many cases profitable private companies, and then of course you are going to grow. When the bull market ends, as it did abruptly on 19 October 1987, your share price crashes, probably further than those of more mundane stocks, because everyone realizes the party, especially your party, is over – and it is. Just as your growth was self-fulfilling, so is your stagnation. The real test comes then – are you truly as good as you thought you were (and as the market thought you were) at running the companies you bought so cheaply with your expensive paper?

The classic shell

Sorrell and a stockbroker at Henderson & Crosthwaite, Preston Rabl, bought a stake in this little shopping trolley manufacturer called Wire and Plastic Products. It was a classic 'shell', a company with a public quote and a small capitalization where one could buy a significant, preferably controlling, stake and inject other profitable businesses. In June 1985 they paid £516,000 for a 27% stake at 38p. Not surprisingly,

THE BBC BOMB

PAPER
FIREWORKS

Sorrell: bull market whizz-kid or international tycoon?

news of this purchase leaked out. After all, if you think you're a whizz-kid and you're planning to use your paper you want everyone to know it so they'll buy the paper. WPP shares immediately rose to 50p, but there for some weeks the price stuck.

Our stockbroker Charles is watching all this, knows of Rabl's involvement and does nothing. He thinks he has probably missed most of the action – the shares have risen by 30% very quickly. He neither buys any for PA nor does he advise any of his clients to do so. Peter was not too pleased about that when he discussed it with him later. In fact as the price climbs – it is 300p by the end of

1985, 600p by the middle of 1986 and 1,000p by early 1987 – Charles feels constantly that he has missed the boat. No one will ever have missed the same boat quite so many times!

By early 1987 it was now worth between £13 and £14 million. Heady stuff – and it gave Sorrell and his backers, those institutions again, the guts to go for one of the oldest established advertising agencies in the world, J. Walter Thompson. J. Walter must have been turning in his grave. Armed with the Ford account, he had marched out from Madison Avenue all over the world, and now his company was being taken over by an unknown English company which two years earlier had been making supermarket trolleys. Anyway, JWT went down faster than Goliath, and the good old institutions swallowed a great deal of WPP paper to finance the deal. It caused some indigestion as the market wobbled in the summer of 1987 and severe stomach pains as it crashed in October – the price came back to 303, having reached a high in early 1987 of 1112.

Could he run the companies?

This was the test for Sorrell. His paper was still expensive, PE in the twenties but not stratospheric. Furthermore, a lot of institutions were now 'stuffed' with it and it had been bought at much higher prices. Could he run all the companies he had bought? And most important, could he cut costs at JWT and produce the increased margins he had promised? We shall see. If he can, he moves up from bull market whizz-kid to Successful International Tycoon. He was not helped in his ambitions by six top executives in one of his leading US agencies walking out one morning in the spring of '88 – a classic case of the assets going down in the lift one evening and not coming back in the morning.

Takeovers

Darren sighs. He knows all the signs. When a client comes on the phone and says, 'Buy me 10,000 Carless. They're definitely going to be taken over. The deal's going to be announced at 9.30 on Wednesday,' Darren knows that the price is being ramped and that there is no chance of any such deal happening. On the other hand, when one of his mates tells him he has noticed friends of the shrewder operators buying then Darren sits up straight.

> **RAMP** It is possible for a group of investors to ramp a share either up or down by acting together and effectively creating a false market by giving the rest of the punters the impression that there are either more sellers or more buyers around than there really are.

One of the greatest ramps ever was put through by Nathan Rothschild in 1815 when he had advance information (as Gordon Gekko says, information is king) that Wellington had won the Battle of Waterloo. Initially Rothschild sold a little stock – ostentatiously – and was followed by everyone else, driving prices down. He then bought – less ostentatiously – and when news of the victory came through and prices rocketed he made a killing.

A more recent example was Bud Fox's organization of his friends in the film *Wall Street* to ramp the price of the airline Blue Star, in order to get back at Gordon Gekko who had shown him how to do it in the first place.

Takeovers are the really exciting part of stock market investment. That's where people think all the insider dealing goes on

and where they would love to have the information themselves. It's amazing how the prices of companies that are bid for rise in the weeks before a bid is announced. Someone knew – of course someone knew – and someone bought, and there's nothing quite like buying – particularly determined buying – to push up prices.

Takeover at its raunchiest

Miles of print have already been written about the Guinness scandal and miles more will be written. In essence it encapsulates the worst elements of the City – greed, the pursuit of power, deceit, insider dealing, chicanery, cowardice – you name it, it had it. The so-called Establishment were involved, perhaps unwittingly – David Mayhew of Cazenove was in Ernest Saunders' War Cabinet. The muck-rakers were involved – Bells' chairman, Raymond Miquel, was physically threatened, as was his daughter. The not-so-nice element of City PR came to the fore when someone passed on to the press the information that Jimmy Gulliver's stay at Harvard Business School had been a mere three weeks.

PUSHING UP THE PRICE

IS GUINNESS GOOD FOR YOU?

This was takeover at its raunchiest. The money was big. One morning the merchant bankers Samuel Montagu and Charterhouse gave their broker an order to buy 115 million Distillers shares at 660p. Whichever way you look at it, that is £700 million. Even so it was not enough. The price had risen above 660p. The overseas element was there. Tom Ward, an American lawyer, was at Saunders' elbow telling all and sundry to cut the crap out. The mandatory Swiss banks were there both buying stock on behalf of British clients and receiving money paid out to various participants in the drama.

Unpleasant advertising

Nothing in takeover situations was ever going to be the same after the Guinness takeover of Distillers. Full-page advertisements in the national press denigrating the opposition had become a common and increasingly unpleasant feature of contested

bids. The Takeover Panel put a stop to it. The buying of the bidder's shares to keep up the price and so keep up the value of the offer had become increasingly common. In the Guinness takeover it reached mammoth proportions. The practice will be carefully vetted in the future.

Broken promises

Promises made in takeover documents were broken. In future they will scarcely be believed. We learnt what a 'poison pill' was when Guinness extracted the guarantee from Distillers that they would pay Guinness's takeover costs if they lost and Argyll won. Argyll naturally protested about this, but were over-ruled by the Takeover Panel. The pill eventually reached the size of £50 million.

The leveraged bid

One element of the Guinness scandal which was new and not necessarily scandalous, though some did not like it, was the arrival of the leveraged bid. Until the eighties takeover bids were made by larger companies for smaller companies. Indeed until Sigmund Warburg's famous organization of the TI/Reynolds bid for British Aluminium in the fifties there were no contested bids.

But now both in the City and on Wall Street the whizz-kids started to dream up bids for the small good 'un so that he could take over the big bad 'un. Many big bad 'uns had grown fat and lazy after takeover sprees of their own in the sixties and seventies, and they had become a ragbag of businesses without the synergy which had been much trumpeted at the time of the takeover. Corporate raiders could see that they could buy such lazy guys, break them up, keep the best and flog the rest. But how to raise the cash in the first place?

> **LEVERAGED BID** A bid for a company where the predator is borrowing money to make that bid.

Satellite press conferences

This was where the new-style merchant banks came in. The first such bid that really captured the imagination, mainly because of the characters involved, was the attack by the Australian John Elliott of Elders IXL on the sleepy Allied Lyons chaired by Derrick Holden-Brown. Allied was a large company with a host of household names as brands, valued at £2 billion. Elders' market value was only £520 million. At first Allied treated the bid as some sort of joke, but Elliott was deadly serious. He toured the City and held satellite press conferences from Australia telling the institutions how he had built up Elders. Neither the public nor most of the institutions for that matter had ever heard of Elders, but they knew its most famous product, ice-cold Foster's lager, thanks to a brilliant series of Pommy-bashing ads featuring Paul Hogan.

Elliott told them he was going to flog off all the non-drinks pieces of Allied to repay the money he borrowed to buy Allied in the first place. It was new – although 15 years earlier Jim Slater used to get into trouble for borrowing money against a company's assets so that he could buy shares in that company – but it looked as though it was going to work.

Wee Jimmy Gulliver

Others were watching and learning, not least wee Jimmy Gulliver of Argyll. The son of a grocer from Campbeltown on the west coast of Scotland, he had built up the Argyll Group in a serious of audacious moves. Now he wanted the big one, the one that would

establish him in Scotland: Distillers. The only trouble was, Distillers was big. It may have been appallingly run and therefore not growing, but it was still much bigger than Argyll. Jimmy felt he needed a powerful partner, and thought he had found one in the slightly unlikely person of Arnold Weinstock of GEC. Actually he had been led there by Lazards, and Lazards had come to Jimmy via Sir Ian MacGregor. Sir Ian just happened to have an estate in Scotland next to Gulliver's.

So wee Jimmy was going to bid for Distillers, and the mighty GEC with their notorious £1.5 billion cash mountain was going to support him. What went wrong? According to Ivan Fallon in the *Sunday Times*, Weinstock wanted to go racing instead of talking to Gulliver. According to Peter Grant, the deputy chairman of

KEEP THE BEST FLOG THE REST

The famous face of Elders: Paul Hogan bashes the Pommies

Sir Thomas Risk, left, caught in the trap; James Gulliver, centre, rejected; Ernest Saunders, right, soon to land in court

Lazards, who presumably had a better inside track than Fallon, Weinstock was deliberately unavailable because he was unhappy with Gulliver and the terms of the deal. Gulliver then uttered what could be the most expensive sentence in modern City history: 'We do not intend to make an offer for Distillers at the present time.'

An ill-considered remark

In that case, said the Takeover Panel, you cannot make one for three months. That ill-considered remark of Gulliver's was bad for him but good for Distillers shareholders. When he made it the Distillers share price was 350p and the company was valued at £1.2 billion. An offer then of 450p or £1.6 billion might have won the day. It would almost certainly have precluded Guinness from bidding, as they had only just completed their purchase of Bells. As it was, three months later Argyll opened with an

offer of 513p or £1.8 billion, and Distillers was finally knocked down for 672p or £2.36 billion.

Clangers apart, Argyll was eventually able to bid – Samuel Montagu and Charterhouse replaced Lazards as Argyll's advisers, and a clever scheme was put together by Rupert Faure Walker, a corporate finance director, and his boss at Samuel Montagu, Ian Macintosh. Gulliver needed £1.8 billion and his own company was valued at £670 million. How was he going to get it? Like this:

1. £600 million of loan finance, the risk being taken by four banks: Samuel Montagu themselves, Charterhouse Japhet, Royal Bank of Scotland, the Midland and Citibank. These banks agreed to provide an eight-year loan at a receiving rate of 0.35% over the London Inter-Bank Offered Rate (Libor) between years one and five. In years six to eight the rate would rise to 0.5%. If the bid failed, or was referred to the Monopolies Commission, they would be receiving a much lower than normal commitment fee.

2. A £500 million underwriting from a group of six leading institutions before the bid was launched.

3. Another £700 million committed by Samuel Montagu and Charterhouse when the bid was announced.

There would be the same premium on success – and there's the rub. The underwriting fee would be 3% if successful, 1% higher than normal. If it failed or were referred, they would receive one-eighth of 1%. Why would the institutions go along with this? They expected their pound of flesh, come what may. But this was the new macho world – in a bid this size no institution wanted to be left out.

The Takeover Panel

With so much at stake in takeovers – money, jobs, pride – it is hardly surprising that people play to win and never mind how. Up until the late sixties no one seemed to mind how, but at that time, the famous warehousing era of Slater Walker and its acolytes, some of the activities went too far even for hardened City players, and 1969 brought the creation of the City Panel on Takeovers and Mergers. The City knew that if it did not do something to police itself the government would do it for them.

The Takeover Panel has virtually no power in law, and it only worked as well as it did for as long as it did because operators in the City accepted it as the final arbiter. It was only when the macho boys came along in the eighties that its rulings were constantly challenged. By '85 and '86 when the mega-bids arrived – Elders v. Allied, Burtons v. Debenhams, Dixons v. Currys, Hanson v. Imperial, Guinness v. Argyll over Distillers – the Panel was trying to react to

events that had already happened and about which it could only offer empty phrases. Nevertheless it did what it could. It put a stop to the unpleasant and wasteful advertising. Guinness was spending £1 million a week telling the public the good things it would do for Distillers and the bad things Argyll would do. It even took space in the *Sun* and the *Star*. It constantly hauled Morgan Grenfell up before its executive panel, though not always to good effect. For example, when Guinness bid for Bells their advisers turned out to be Morgan Grenfell. Bells, in the rotund form of the voluble Lord Spens, complained to the Panel on the grounds that Morgan Grenfell had been advisers to Bells for years and were privy to all Bells' thoughts, plans etc. How could they act for Guinness?

Overstepping the mark

Grenfell had probably overstepped the mark – they would be reprimanded, but could continue acting for Guinness. Spens was not accepting this and asked for a meeting of the full Panel. Bells were

POLICE WITH NO POWER

Battle of the ad campaigns

**Sir Ralph Halpern: a
bull in a bear market**

put forward their appeal and finally Morgan
Grenfell were asked to comment. Morgan
Grenfell pointed out that Bells had only
spent £20,000 with them in the last two
years and that Guinness would now be
paying them £6 million.

Having heard the evidence, everyone
was asked to retire while the Panel
deliberated. Such deliberations can take
several hours. Lord Spens recalls it took
three minutes. All were summoned back,
and Saunders and Ward were now with
Reeves and Walsh. Spens objected to this.
Sir Jasper Hollom then gave his judgement.
Morgan Grenfell had no case to answer.
Furthermore the Panel's earlier censure of
the bank was withdrawn.

In theory all bids are put forward as a
vital link in a well-thought strategy of
industrial logic to provide commercial synergy. Rubbish! In fact most bids happen
because a company, or more usually one
man, wants to be richer and more powerful.
The fact that in many but by no means all
cases this process has a beneficial effect in
increasing efficiency is just a happy
coincidence.

Where's the synergy?

If you think there is great synergy
between Debenhams and Burtons and that
it's all a big team event, name one other
director apart from Sir Ralph Halpern. You
might have wondered also how it was that
the problems Guinness found in the Distillers Company were so great that Sir
Thomas Risk had to be ditched as chairman.
One man, Ernest Saunders, was now supposed to combine the roles of chairman and
chief executive and have his finger on every
button. Amazingly, when the authorities
arrived for a chat a few months later this
omnipotent CEO knew nothing of the shen-
anigans going on under each mighty digit.

represented by Raymond Miquel and Henry
King as directors of the company, by Lord
Spens and by Roger Court of Henry Ansb-
acher, the merchant bank drafted in to
advise them, and by the lawyers Herbert
Smith. Morgan Grenfell were represented
by Christopher Reeves and Graham Walsh
(an ex-Director General of the Panel), both
subsequently dismissed from the bank. In
attendance were Ernest Saunders and the
American lawyer Tom Ward (both under
arrest at the time of writing).

The Panel presented their case, then Bells

Privatization

There never was much love lost between Margaret Thatcher and Harold Macmillan, later Lord Stockton, particularly as Mrs T felt that Macmillan set in train the type of government policy which accelerated Britain's decline. Macmillan's formative years were heavily influenced by the slaughter in the trenches of the First World War and the further slaughter of man's dignity in the slums of his one-time constituency of Stockton-on-Tees – the closest most of his chums got to Stockton was flying over it on their way to shoot grouse.

As a result of these influences Macmillan, supported by the family's publishing fortune and further supported by the assets of his wife's family, the Devonshires, felt that money should be given to the deserving masses whenever they asked for it. That way the masses would be content and he and his chums could enjoy the life to which they had been born. Clearly he had not read his firm's book on Eva Peron. She gave money to the poor, failing to realize that printing money and giving it to people only makes them better off on the very shortest of timescales – in Macmillan's Britain a matter of weeks, in Peron's Argentina a matter of days, in 1920s' Germany a matter of seconds.

Printing money means inflation, and inflation means unemployment. Milton Friedman understood it. He taught Thatcher. Thatcher has almost taught the rest of us. She must have been mightily miffed when Macmillan, in referring to her grand plan for giving money away in a non-inflationary (well almost) way, made one of his clever laid-back speeches about giving away the family silver.

SELLING THE FAMILY SILVER

BT investors buy their shares on the spot. They couldn't get through on the phone.

PRIVATIZING THE SLAVE TRADE

The South Sea Bubble

Was it a new idea? It was not. The British government had done it before, as long ago as 1720. That government also made loud noises about worthy reasons for flogging shares to the people. In 1720 it was opening up trade with South America, in the 1980s it was making British Telecom more efficient (pardon?) and more aware of their customers (really?). In both cases it was, of course, to rid themselves of public debt.

If you think you did well out of the flotations of British Telecom, British Gas, British This and British That, your great-great-great-great-great-great-great-great-grandfather did much better out of the flotation of the South Sea Company. Provided, of course, he got out before the bubble burst.

Mesmerized by success

Set up in 1711 by the government, the company did very little for eight years except supply black slaves to Latin America – this was a year or two before the Race Relations Acts – but then in 1719 it was decided to offer shares to the general public. The PR man who masterminded the promotion, the Dewe Rogerson of the era, was Sir John Blunt. Guess what: you only had to pay a little at the start and the rest by instalments. The issue was heavily over-subscribed, and there was an outcry when it was discovered that men of influence had received an extra allocation. You may think *this* government is greedy, but they are as suckling babes compared with their predecessors. In 1719, mesmerized by their success, the government made loans to the public secured on the shares themselves provided the money was used to buy more stock. It's not the sort of deal NatWest would readily countenance. If this was not the fuel for a short-lived boom and then a mighty Crash it is difficult to think of a better one. Pouring oil on the flames was the oleaginous Blunt, who talked of high dividends and the ending of the war with Spain.

Infamous corruption

British Telecom shares doubled on the first day of dealings and moved up another 50% or so in the following few weeks before becoming steady and relatively dull. Shares in the South Sea Company stood at £128 in early 1720. By March they were £330, by May £550 and by 24 June £1,050. Boom! At that point the government, after all its members had sold at or near the peak, brought in an Act to prevent similar enterprises. Crash! Within weeks the price was back to £175 and by the end of the year it was £124, slightly lower than the starting price. There was, of course, an enquiry. There always is. It discovered that some ministers had indeed 'not answered their telephones', and the Chancellor of the

Exchequer, the Duke of Argyll, was found guilty of 'infamous corruption' and sent to the Tower. The whole episode triggered a bear market which lasted for a century.

Could the government have fallen?

It is interesting to speculate what might have happened to Chancellor Lawson if the Crash of '87 had come just ten days later, when everyone's application for BP shares would have been posted and people would have been stuffed with shares at 120p which would have opened at 70p if they were lucky or possibly 40p if they tried to sell. Certainly Lawson would have been sacrificed as Leon Brittan was, and it is not too fanciful to imagine the government falling. Sid may not be a revolutionary, but he does not like to be made to look a proper Charlie on that scale, or so publicly.

Use your Swiss bank

On Sid's behalf the government and its advisers were doing some incredibly stupid things. In the Telecom issue the British private investor received 800 shares, whatever he or she applied for. The only exceptions were MP Keith Best, who made several applications; and anyone who applied from overseas – for example a private application from Britain through a Swiss bank for 20,000 shares received an allocation of 10,000 shares. The same application via Lloyds in Esher or Canterbury would have received 800. The difference in profit on day one was £5,000 as opposed to £400, and within a month was £10,000 as opposed to £800. Unbelievably, the government allocated more to American institutions than they wanted and half was sent back. The government was unsure whether to congratulate itself on saving the £100 million on the one half or to institute an enquiry into

SID – THE POPULAR CAPITALIST

Sid's a retired insurance clerk. Having a little spare cash in the early eighties, he decided to dabble in some small investments. He has bought TSB shares, British Telecom, British Gas (after much teasing by his mates back home in Birmingham, who don't all share his working-class Tory principles) and Virgin, after his granddaughter kept on saying how 'brilliant' she thought the company was. He is a little circumspect about Virgin, thinking it might be slightly rude, especially as they sell those balloons he used to play with as a squaddie in his army days. His portfolio now totals appreciably over £1,750 and he enjoys talking about 'my stockbroker' in the Conservative Club.

An enthusiastic investor displays the head-butt technique in share applications

the instant £100 million it had given away on the other half.

The Britoil fiasco

The really crass performance came with the next privatization, the 49% government stake in Britoil. The issue of the first half in 1982 had been a flop, and the government decided with this one to pitch the price very low and to reserve only 15% for the public. The rest were allocated to institutions, both British and foreign, who could scarcely believe their luck. Worse was to follow. The public apply for new issues if newspapers, especially the *Daily Telegraph*, tell them to. In this case they did and they did. The allocation system was little short of ridiculous and seemed to have been dreamt up by someone who was completely unaware of even the basics of the stock market.

Those who applied for between 200 and 1,100 shares received 100, those applying for between 1,200 and 1,400 received 150, and those appallingly wealthy people who applied for more than 1,400 received none at all. Our friend with the Swiss bank account received whatever he applied for. It was beyond belief – an American pension fund could have thousands, but a British doctor could have none. The conglomerate Pearson did not have a consistent corporate view – its merchant bank, Lazards, which made millions out of handling the sale, described the issue as 'a great success'. Its newspaper, the *Financial Times*, preferred to use words like 'fiasco' and 'con'. A leading corporate

financier suggested that the prospectus was misleading. He felt it should have said: 'If you apply for more than 1,400 shares and the flotation is successful you will get none. If, however, it's a flop we'll stuff you with your full application.'

Everyone very quickly got bored with the mythical Sid, but they also, it has to be admitted, obeyed their masters and applied for shares in the next big state sell-off, British Gas. This time the allocations division was a little better. Though not large, they were not derisory, and the 'fat plutocrat who didn't deserve any' level was raised to 100,000. Gas was a success, as were British Airways, Rolls Royce and British Airports Authority. Then came the big one, and the government was now into share-

pushing at a level which, if practised by individuals, would quickly bring legislation to outlaw it. BP was actually advertised as though it was molten gold. By this time almost the whole population who could read and scrape together a few hundred quid were going to apply.

£60 million of advertising

£23 million was spent on ads, which brought the total amount spent on advertising the privatization issues to £60 million. But just as everyone was preparing to send in an application we had Meltdown, and the BP share price melted with it. Everyone who applied was guaranteed to lose 50p on every share. It would have been more, but Chancellor Lawson made the

Commandos abseil down Britannic House to warn BP investors of what is to come

The happy face of a BP investor who got his shares just in time

Bank of England offer to buy back the 120p shares at 70p – the fastest ever renationalization of any enterprise. Nevertheless an incredible 250,000 people applied for shares – 'You don't want to believe what you read in the papers, the government will see us right' was presumably the attitude. This is surely the most valuable mailing list of suckers in the UK. Astoundingly, there were even some multiple applications. The authorities didn't know whether to prosecute them or give them medals.

Squealing like stuck pigs

The underwriters (those who had guaranteed to take a certain number of shares whatever happened) squealed like stuck pigs, especially the Americans. This was 1987, not 1984, and the American financial institutions had now caught on to the fact that the wunnerful Maggie Thatcher was giving away all those Limey utilities. Underwriting as big a chunk as you could

get was a sure-fire way to make a few million bucks. Having made the few million with increasing enthusiasm on British Gas, British Airways etc. they applied to underwrite as many of the BP issue as they could and then lost those millions and more when the issue flopped. It's not only private investors who need to be told that shares can go down as well as up. In the event the ones that showed real guts, or was it just common sense, were the Kuwaitis, who bought 22% through the Kuwait Investment Office. Ultimately the government decided they didn't like this and referred it to the MMC.

Thatcher should watch out

If Thatcher and Lawson are not careful, all those extra 7 million Sid-type shareholders so carefully created since 1979, and who voted for them so gleefully in June 1987, will be voting for Kinnock in 1992. Looking at the prices of their shares in British Telecom, British Gas, British Airports Authority and British Airways, they'll realize that his promise to nationalize them all again and give the shareholders their money back without the unpleasant surprise of the new dealing costs can only be a good thing.

The new financial supermarkets brought lower prices for the big buyers, certainly. For Peter and Sid, no. On deals over £50,000 commission rates fell by as much as 50%. On small deals for the private investor, however, the phrase 'minimum commission' was heard more frequently, and every time Sid heard it it had gone up a fiver. Of course there were lots of tempting offers initially, particularly from the high street banks: 'We'll sell your British Gas shares for only £5.' But soon the £5 had become £25, and when you were selling £250 worth, £25 or 10% in commission, plus VAT of course, was making the 1.65% of pre-Big Bang days look pretty good.

Nobody wants Sid

The truth is that Sid is a pain in the arse to the new financial conglomerates. The allocations in most of these privatizations were ridiculously small, so that now there are millions of punters with 150 of this and 200 of that. If you add the whole lot together it seldom comes to more than £2,000. Suppose he wants to sell any of them, or even all of them. How much will the broker earn out of the dealings – £25? Wow. Sid may even lose most of the profit he has made on the shares when you take into account the dealing cost and some accountant's time in calculating it all to find out what the capital gains/losses tax position is, even if the answer is that there is no tax liability because it is under the limit.

Better off at the Abbey

Sid should either have left his money in the traditional dull haven of the building society or he should have put his pennies in unit trusts. Twenty years ago he would have been quite happy with the building society.

> **UNIT TRUST** A trust formed to manage securities on behalf of a number of small investors.

Indeed he would not have known of any other investment medium. When the great inflation robbery of the 1970s came along he realized that unit trusts offered him some protection against his money depreciating at 10, 15 or even 20% a year. If he settles for unit trusts rather than individual shares his broker will love him because he'll get the 3% commission paid to him by unit trusts instead of the 1.65% for investing directly,

and Sid himself, except on days like 19 October 1987, will probably get a better deal when he tries to redeem his money. There's no doubt about it. Whatever happens between now and 1991, either that year or 1992 will witness another bull market because the government dare not risk losing the votes of all those disgruntled new shareholders.

Nigel Lawson shows the caring face of popular capitalism

-5- *SIDE PLAYERS*

TOP DOWN BOTTOM UP

Journalists

Sir Patrick Sergeant, *Private Eye*'s favourite financial journalist, used to be the share tipster on the *Daily Mail*. Tipsters have no small opinion of their abilities, and he once made the mistake of advising his readers not to buy or sell while he was on holiday. When he got back he found a telegram from the gigantic Prudential Assurance Company: 'Now you are back, can we buy?'

There are effectively two types of financial journalist. One wants to give you the impression he knows something no one else knows because he has been specially treated by a certain company or is especially clever.

This, of course, can run perilously close to inside information.

The other type of financial journalist is the thinker who equates with those who buy a share because the fundamentals of the company are sound, and who couldn't care less whether the chairman gets into the office at 6 a.m. or spends all night on the town.

The dilemma is to choose between macro – in City jargon Top Down: the study of broad economic and political circumstances and trends; and micro, i.e. Bottom Up, ignore the trends, this company's a buy.

Plenty of stories

Financial journalists need never worry about being short of a story. A whole new industry has emerged in the last few years whose sole function is to influence, if necessary write, what goes into those columns. When Peter, our private investor, reads on Sunday that Property Trust is going places, he can hardly wait until Monday morning to buy 20,000. Peter does not realize two things. First, the tip has probably come via a PR company who fed it to the newspaper (this is so regular that it is known as the Friday Night Drop). The market-makers who make a market in Property Trust can read too and are waiting for Peter. What was 6p on Friday is now 9p. Peter and all the other Peters don't care – what's another 3p when the company's going to be used as a shell and the price is going to £1? The market-makers don't have millions of Property Trust on their book, but they still sell at 9p knowing they can buy them when the price falls back on Wednesday and Thursday. What seemed a great idea on Sunday does not look so good by the following Thursday. In his excitement Peter failed to notice that 9p is 50% more than 6p. If he had been tipped to buy ICI at £10 he would hardly have expected to pay £15 the next morning.

PR

But this is being unkind to financial PR companies, to the newspapers that print their stories and to the market-makers who eat Peter for breakfast every Monday morning. There are many respectable financial PR companies who do an excellent job in portraying what solid companies they work for, and therefore what a sound investment a purchase of their shares would be. By and large this is their main function, and a lot of the work is fairly routine. What makes the blood run a little faster are the takeover battles or the big issues such as the privatization programme.

What do the shareholders think?

Obviously, in a takeover the predator and potential victim feel very strongly about their respective cases, and are playing to win. They expect their advisers to do the same, and in the case of a contested bid involving public companies what happens to share prices can be most important, even critical. What happens to the share prices or whether shareholders sell their shares in a bid situation can be influenced, indeed will be influenced, by what those shareholders think of the companies. That is where the PR advisers come in, and indeed should have been coming in for years before. When Guinness bid for Bells, Saunders made all

the right PR moves, flew immediately to Scotland to brief Scottish journalists and cultivated the Charlotte Square mafia. Miquel, the Bells' chairman, made all the wrong ones – he failed to return immediately from the United States, when he did he held his first press conference in London instead of Edinburgh, and he publicly shouted at a TV technician. The images that came over were that Bells was badly run, which was wrong, and that Guinness was well run, which also turned out to be wrong.

INFLUENTIAL ADVICE

Two patient messengers awaiting orders

DIGGING UP THE DIRT

In bid battles the PR work can be clean, concentrating on the merits of the bid or the defence, or it can be dirty, with boardroom bugging, the investigation of key personnel and – this was a very low point for the industry – the revelation to a Sunday newspaper that the chairman of a company had made an inaccurate *Who's Who* entry. During Dixons' attempt to take over Woolworth they resorted to employing private detectives to snoop into the private lives of Woolworth executives. When they were found out, Dixons' bland excuse was that the surveillance was 'to ascertain the senior directors' suitability for future employment within the Dixons Group, in the event that the bid succeeded'. As Dixons' report on Woolworth chairman Geoffrey Mulcahy regretfully commented that 'We were unable to find anything to the family's detriment', it does seem to have been a remarkably in-depth recruitment drive.

Occupying power

PR charges per hour are quite steep, effectively four times whatever the PR executive is being paid. If you are employing a top man, therefore, who might well be paid £100,000 a year, expect to pay £200 an hour for him. For a lesser mortal you can halve that.

You can start a PR company very easily from scratch, and with good contacts and lots of balls you can make it big. You probably need to be imaginative in your early days, as was the chairman of one of the agencies when he was visited by a potential client who clearly thought he was bigger than he actually was. In fact the PR company occupied two rooms of a large building owned by an advertising agency. The chairman persuaded the people in the ad agency to go to lunch, and then used their boardroom and their office. With his few employees sprinting from office to office, across the fire escapes and through the window, he managed to give the impression that he occupied the whole building. He didn't catch the client, but it does not seem to have held him back as Peter Gummer's Shandwick is now the biggest PR company in this country, and with his continuing acquisitions abroad seems well on his way to becoming the biggest in the world.

Solicitors

The biggest firm of City solicitors is Clifford Chance, the sleekest is Slaughter & May, and the one with the best advice on the USM is Nabarro Nathanson.

Lawyers are not as omniscient in British

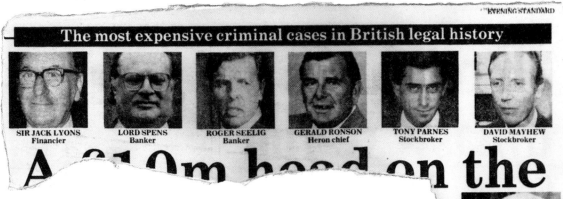

EVENING STANDARD

The most expensive criminal cases in British legal history

| SIR JACK LYONS | LORD SPENS | ROGER SEELIG | GERALD RONSON | TONY PARNES | DAVID MAYHEW |
| Financier | Banker | Banker | Heron chief | Stockbroker | Stockbroker |

A £10m head on the

corporate finance work as they are in New York, but there is usually one around once anything significant is happening, whether it is raising some money, considering a bid or fighting off a bid. It is difficult to find a poor lawyer anywhere and you certainly won't find one in the City. An assistant solicitor in his thirties will earn at least £30,000, and once he becomes a partner in a major firm he can think about the magic six-figure salary. As a senior partner he will be taking advice himself on how to hold on to as much as possible of his £200,000-300,000.

Don't waste money on trees

If you are lucky enough to be paying for the privilege of hearing the wise words of these well-paid counsellors it will cost you about £150 an hour for the assistant solicitor, £200 an hour for the partner and God knows what for one of the top guys like Simon Ward at Slaughter & May, who headed up the team that handled the BT flotation.

Not that you will be over-awed by the opulence of their offices. You won't have to fight your way through foliage as you now have to in the atriums of the banks and stockbrokers. Slaughter & May's office at Basinghall Street is almost drab, and you will be seen in a modest interview room. But then you wouldn't want to gain the impression that any of the whacking fee you are going to pay was being wasted on unusual Brazilian trees or antique furniture.

Taking over the small hours

As with other areas of the City, it's the takeovers that get the adrenalin flowing, when the lads work all through the night. Slaughter & May have just put sleeping accommodation into their offices. All the new legislation to try to check the worst excesses of the City will of course be a bonanza for the legal eagles – first drafting them, then explaining them, and finally interpreting them.

ERNEST SAUNDERS
Ex-Guinness chairman

Accountants

As the City is all about money there are thousands of accountants about the place. They don't do anything different in the City from anywhere else. They keep the score, as was made only too clear by the chairman of a Yorkshire textile company who was interrupted at an AGM by his auditor. 'Nay, lad,' said the chairman. 'Sit down. Tha's just the scorer!'

Evening Standard, **1 June 1988**

-6- *THE DOWNSIDE*

A NUDGE IS AS GOOD AS A WINK

Insider Dealing

We all love inside information when we are on the inside and condemn it when we are on the outside. The old-style stockbroker like Charles relied on inside tips and winks to supplement his already considerable income. Unfortunately the nouveaux got greedy and did not keep their mouths shut, with the result that government made it first illegal and then in 1980 a criminal offence. It is, however, notoriously difficult to prove in a court of law. After all, without a confession how does the law prove that Charles's purchase of Bells stock just before Guinness bid for them was not just a rare good idea? Let's take an imaginary example and show how profitable acting on inside information can be.

In June 1985 Schumacher were about to bid for Bond Electronics. In April that year Bond's share price was 130p. When Harry Schumacher launched his bid on Friday, 14 June, apparently prompted by a sharp rise in four days from 160p to 192p, the shares moved ahead to 225p. Charles had worked

out that further rationalization was overdue in the electronics business and invested £10,000 in Bond in April. That bought him 7,500 shares, and when he sold them in June he received about £16,500 – not a bad little earner for having used his nous.

How to use the inside track

But insider dealers do not work in such modest little ways. In April Gerard knew there was going to be a bid because he just happened to be working on the deal. He also knew, unlike Darren's friend who can apparently time the conclusion of such deals to the very minute, that these things can take time and that they can fall apart. Still, on balance he felt this one would go through. The way to benefit in a big way was by taking a call option and gearing himself up, but he decided to be just a little cautious in case the deal broke down. Gerard decided to punt £100,000, so he bought 50,000 shares which cost him £66,000, and a three-month call option – this gave him the right to buy a fixed number of shares at a specified price within this period of time – at a striking price of 131, which

cost him just over £30,000 for 200,000 at the option price of 15p. He reckoned that if the bid fell through or did not take place within three months, the traditional period for options, he would still have his 50,000 shares, and he was certain the price would move up while the bid was still being planned. After all, he was in a position to tell enough people to make sure that it did.

As April soaked into May, the bid looked more and more certain and Gerard, bolder now, decided to buy another 200,000 on option. This time he had to pay 16p and the striking price was 140p. By the time June came it was a dead cert and he had a final fling, taking yet another option on 200,000, paying 20p with a striking price of 180 and buying 50,000 shares at 180 'for the account'.

Totting up the score

When the bid is announced and the price moves to 225p, Gerard has made stockbroker Charles's little coup look just that. Little.

Let's tot up Gerard's score:

50,000 shares bought at 130 and sold at 225
  Profit: £47,500

200,000 shares bought at 131 and sold at 225
  Profit 188,000 less 200,000 × 15p
  option money: £158,000

200,000 shares bought at 140 and sold at 225
  Profit 170,000 less 200,000 × 16p
  option money: £138,000

200,000 shares bought at 180 and sold at 225
  Profit 90,000 less 200,000 × 20p
  option money: £50,000

50,000 shares bought at 180 and sold at 225
  Profit: £22,500

Total profit before costs   £416,000

GERARD – THE INSIDER DEALER

Gerard, born in north London, educated at Westminster, is the ace whizzer – fast thinking, fast talking, fast dealing and completely amoral, he likes to be seen to be successful. Just under 40, he was the star at his merchant bank, where the emphasis was always supposed to be on the team. Everyone thinks he is very clever and everyone loathes him, particularly his wife, who is now living with a literary agent in Primrose Hill. On the rare occasions when he takes his girlfriend to the theatre, he books three seats – the extra one's for his portable phone.

GERARD MAKES A KILLING

The capital outlay, while not negligible, was not as great as you might think. It was £66,000 for the first lot of shares, just over £100,000 for the options, and nothing for the last lot of shares. Never mind the scale, the return on it was certainly better than Charles's.

But, you may ask, what has happened to all the new regulations about insider dealing and the 1980 Act making it a criminal offence, and the compliance officers at all the City institutions? Gerard bypassed all those by dealing from – no, not Switzerland, even that's not safe these days, but from the Caribbean where no one can trace the ownership of shares.

A slap on the wrist

The really criminal thing about insider dealing in this country in the eighties (insider dealing is not even illegal in Japan – indeed they cannot think of any other reason to buy a stock) is that when a senior City figure had been caught red-handed and pleaded guilty the judge, Mr Justice Farquharson, let him off with a £25,000 fine. Geoffrey Collier, whose salary in November 1986 as joint managing director of Morgan Grenfell Securities was £70,000 plus a guaranteed bonus of £50,000, and who enjoyed share options and other perks, was able to walk out of court with that fine after admitting to assets of over £700,000. That was perhaps the most incredible aspect of his case, but there were others.

It was understood that Morgan Grenfell had paid him a large Golden Hallo, supposedly over £200,000, and they were of course rewarding him reasonably adequately. At the time of his arrest a total of five cases of his insider dealing were revealed by the *Financial Times* and in three of them he had actually lost money. How could a man be worth that salary, that

bonus, those share options and that Golden Hallo, and still lose money on three out of five deals in a roaring bull market when he had inside information? In public the City tut-tutted about his dishonesty, but in private they were much more appalled by his incompetence.

Cocky Collier

In the autumn of 1986 Collier was symbolic of how much certain elements in the City thought they could get away with. After all, his bosses also employed Roger Seelig, and they were constantly being hauled up in front of the Takeover Panel for their conduct in various takeover battles. As nothing worse than a few admonitory remarks ever happened, they began to think they could walk on water. So cocky was Collier that he organized the purchase of shares in a company, AE (Associated Engineering), just before a bid was announced by Robert Maxwell's Hollis Group, which Collier just happened to be advising. Collier organized the purchase from Los Angeles through a former colleague at Vickers da Costa. The purchase was made at 8.30 on a Monday morning, which was 12.30 on Sunday night in Los Angeles, a somewhat strange time to be buying shares in a relatively obscure English company. Market-makers do not like to be made to look suckers, or to lose money, and when Maxwell's offer was announced at 9 a.m. suspicions already aroused were confirmed. Cocky Collier was for the high jump.

Obscene money

The apparently obscene money being made in the City in 1986 and 1987 was becoming the focus of attack from the less prosperous parts of the country and the government was fearful of a backlash which might lose it the election, due in mid-1987.

It was all the more surprising, then, that the judge felt it necessary only to fine Collier. Clearly the QC to retain was Robert Alexander, whose other famous client of 1987 was Jeffrey Archer in his libel case against the *Star* newspaper. Ironically,

The Times, 2 July 1987

WALKING ON WATER

KING OF THE ARBS

Alexander was appointed chairman of the Takeover Panel, and his first court case after this appointment was to defend a self-confessed insider trader.

In view of the lenient treatment of Collier the fate of the barrister and MP Keith Best was surprising. He was given a jail sentence, subsequently rescinded, for making six applications under various versions of his name and from different addresses for shares in British Telecom when it was floated in 1984. The prospectuses of later state sell-offs contained definite warnings of the illegality of such activities, but in the British Telecom prospectus there was only a rather vague warning. Indeed in most issues multiple applications were permissible, even encouraged. Best was treated harshly. In comparing his case with Collier's the inevitable conclusion was that the contacts you had and the lawyer you could afford counted for a lot. In Collier's case, Alexander showed the judge 60 letters from influential financial people from all over the world saying what a nice guy he was. The

> **ARBITRAGEUR (arb)** Someone who buys a significant and therefore influential stake in any company involved in a takeover, in the hope of making a profit from the difference between his purchase price and selling price.

judge believed them and took just 3% of his assets.

Greed is healthy

'Greed is all right. Greed is healthy. You can be greedy and still feel good about yourself.' That was Ivan Boesky talking to City dignitaries in 1986 when he came to London and was received with near adulation. Twelve months later those same people could scarcely remember meeting him. Even as he said it he knew that he, Ivan, King of the Arbs, was being investigated by the authorities in his own country. But the King was resourceful. In return for his co-operation in shopping others he was allowed to sell many of his ill-gotten holdings, surely the biggest case of insider dealing ever.

The unacceptable face of insider trading: Ivan Boesky goes to court

Getting Caught

First and foremost – don't get caught. But if you are, then any one of these nice barristers might be able to mitigate your misery.

Robert Alexander	John Mathew
Robin Auld	Michael Mill
Richard du Cann	Martin Thomas
George Carman	Barney Waylen
Michael Kalisher	

Certain judges are particularly humourless when it comes to City fraud. Theoretically it is not possible to pick and choose your judge. However, if you come up against one of the following, a tactical heart attack (amyl nitrate, digitalis and so on can cause impressive fibrillations – consult your local chemist) may result in proceedings being delayed indefinitely, and eventually reassigned to another judge, or even court. The local City court just happens to be the Old Bailey, the Central Criminal Court, but this is becoming so clogged in this age of growing crime that often City cases are being pushed out into other courts.

Judges to avoid (pop the pill when your name comes up) are as follows:

Old Bailey
His Honour Judge Pigot

Southwark Crown Court
His Honour Judge Butler
His Honour Judge Anwyl-Davis

Inner London Crown Court
His Honour Judge Shindler

Croydon Crown Court
Her Honour Judge Jean Graham-Hall

Isleworth Crown Court
Her Honour Judge Susan Norwood

Master of the Rolls: Tom Pigot, Common Sergeant at the Old Bailey

HOW TO ESCAPE ATTENTION

Wish You Were Here

If it all looks a bit bleak and the word is out that His or Her Honour likes the sound of the words 'Ten years', then you may consider cutting and running. Your passport will already have been removed, but someone with your cool head won't have too much difficulty picking up another, preferably Swiss. This isn't Russia, so your loved ones will eventually be able to follow, but you can say goodbye to the house in Godalming.

But where to go? Spain was popular, but most involuntary British residents in that sunny clime were rather déclassé, often being there because they'd hit somebody too hard. Anyway, now Spain is a member of that rich man's club the EEC, the Spaniards have realized that harbouring criminals is not the done thing and there is an extradition treaty between us and them. Furthermore, the authorities have taken to kicking out those whom they consider undesirable. However, some quiet words about being able to arrange the return of Gibraltar (after all, you are a person of some influence) might persuade them to enjoy the pleasure of your company a little longer.

The USA isn't really any good either. They have tenacious if expensive lawyers who will hold on to you like bulldogs, but there is an extradition treaty and a special relationship and we do swop villains. Flights across the Atlantic are constantly carrying our vice back here and their vice versa.

Exotic tropical islands sound remote enough to escape anyone's attention, but as they were mostly former colonies of ours, we made damn sure that the extradition treaties were in force before we hauled down the flag.

Go for Brazil

South America's the place. Until our recent difference of opinion, Argentina, a country populated by Italians who speak Spanish and think they're Europeans, were determinedly Anglophile. Some of them even play rugby and speak Welsh. Now, of course, if you can get in, the last people the Argentines will listen to a request from is the British government, so you're home and dry. You may, however, encounter a degree of personal animosity.

On the whole, therefore, go for Brazil. You'll be able to meet Ronnie Biggs, the last man to escape from Wandsworth, send postcards to your ex-clients from Copacabana Beach, dance the samba, the bossa nova and the paso doble, and drink exotic rum punches as the sun sets behind you. The weather's great, the girls are beautiful, and the soccer's first-class. Downsides: inflation's awful and there's a large and rather unsavoury criminal element. You should feel right at home. However, if even Brazil is just a poster in a travel agent's window glimpsed through the bars of the Black Maria whisking you away from the court room, take comfort from . . .

Let lawyer Irving David handle your assets in Rio

The City Slicker's Jail Guide

So it's finally happened! After nine months of court appearances, the service of one of the country's leading QCs, and the storm of documents to confuse the jury (three hundredweight of paper entered as evidence), 12 good men and true have found you guilty of fraud – albeit on a majority verdict. But this is a first-past-the-post system, and the judge has sentenced you to three years at Her Majesty's pleasure.

Take heart. This is not as bad as it sounds. There is no need to bite the cyanide capsule, as the financier Whitaker Wright did after being sentenced to seven years for fraud at the Old Bailey. Providing you are a model prisoner (no rooftop protests, *please*!) a third of your sentence will be remitted. You probably didn't spend any time in prison before your case came up, since it was thought unlikely you would rush off and misappropriate £4 million again. All you had to do was to stay every night at your normal address and surrender your passport so you wouldn't take the gentleman's way out (no longer a bullet – nowadays it's through Switzerland to Argentina). They won't have liked you talking to former colleagues – Lord Spens wasn't allowed to when he was granted bail on two sureties of £250,000 in March 1988.

Looking smart at Wandsworth

At the age of 21 Justin Frewin set up Imperial Commodities. Two years later it crashed, taking with it £400,000 of investors' money. The Fraud Squad took an interest, and three years later Justin went to prison. A large amount of media attention was given to Justin because he went to Eton, his uncle is a Viscount, he owned two Rolls-

On yer bike: Justin Frewin pleads his penury

Royces, Prince Andrew once dined at his flat, he was completely bald, he socialized a great deal, he had a very enjoyable time and, lastly, he let the whole world know it.

He began his two-year prison sentence at Wandsworth. The prison issue clothes were not to his liking, so he wore Turnbull & Asser shirts and exchanged his jail boots for a spiffy pair of brogues. As a convicted fraudster he was naturally given the job of collecting and distributing prisoners' wages, and he taught other inmates how to manipulate the computer so the system he devised would work after he left.

Fraudsters are the aristocrats of the prison pecking order (child molesters, unsurprisingly, are at the bottom). The lads' admiration for Justin knew no bounds. His crime became mythical, and the sums involved were inflated into legend. Many were keen to work with him after prison.

The screws also knew a gent when they saw one, and Justin treated them with a courtesy to which they were unaccustomed. They returned the favour. Prison is nothing if not a microcosm of society, and inevitably an Etonian with intelligence, charm, royal associations and a peer for an uncle will float to the top like cream. While inside he wrote a poem, 'The Ballad of Wandsworth Jail', which he now recites at Chelsea dinner parties to besotted young Sloanes, thrilled at meeting such a charming crim.

Back in the slammer: Victorian values triumph

The communal bucket

Initially, after conviction, all prisoners are sent to a secure nick. If your sentence is three years or longer this will probably be Wandsworth. It's a pretty grim place to start with – three to a cell and the communal bucket. You get one hour's exercise a day in the prison yard, and because of overcrowding and the shortage of prison officers the evening 'associations' are getting more rare.

If you are transferred to Long Lartin (which is unlikely) you will be surrounded by plenty of prisoners convicted of violent crime. This is less fun. To offset this you will have your own cell and proper lavatories, and if you have been given more than four years – nice one! – can buy your own food in the canteen and use the kitchenette at the end of each landing. You will earn the money by assembling electronic components. The rate of pay is quite a bit less than you were probably earning in the City – £2.60 a week.

No worse than boarding school

Towards the end of your sentence you might be lucky enough to be sent to Channings Wood, where the food is good and the atmosphere very relaxed. Ford Open Prison is the other likely posting, and if you went to a public school it will probably suit you as it is in the middle of nowhere, the beds are hard, the dormitories are cold and the food appalling. Jonathan Guinness was heard to murmur, after his Eton-educated son Sebastian finished an 11-week sentence in 1987 for his involvement with drugs, 'He lost about six pounds and made a lot of new friends. It wasn't much worse than a term at boarding school.' However, both at Ford and at Springhill near Aylesbury the surrounding countryside is agreeable and you will undoubtedly meet old mates from the City or possibly some chums from school. You may be able to obtain home leave at weekends to visit your loved ones, and daytime leave to go on courses. You can brush up your Italian, or learn motor car maintenance – just the thing for servicing the Porsche now that bills have become something of a problem. One prisoner recently given four years for fraud is allowed out each morning at 7 a.m. and doesn't have to report back until 7 p.m.

The table d'hôte at Ford prison for the last 25 years

-7- THE CRASH OF '87

BLACK MONDAY

Hurricane Friday: the City starts to get windy

By October 1987 the City was wallowing in an orgy of self-love. The Tories were in for another five years, money, serious money was there for the taking, the markets were going up after the usual summer hiccup – then BANG! It all stopped. First New York, then Tokyo and Hong Kong, then London, then New York again, then Hong Kong, Tokyo and Sydney, then London, Paris and Frankfurt all turned into screaming,· yelling pits of hysteria as the markets lost a year's gains in 24 hours. To exacerbate the situation, the hurricane in Britain three days before prevented many dealers from reaching their screens.

It was only 12 years or 3,000 trading days since the FT 30 Index had stood at 147. Now it lost 183.7 in a single day. If we thought that was difficult to cope with, the Dow Jones fell by over 500 points and it was only five years or 1,250 trading days since that index had been around 600. But that of course was part of the reason. The indexes had risen a long way, and once punters wanted to cash in some of their profits there could only be one result. Black Monday, 19 October 1987, was so called after Black Monday on Wall Street in October 1929 – which had itself been named after Black Friday, 24 September 1869, when a group of

punters tried to corner the gold market, causing a panic which led to a crash and a depression.

Breaking all records

So many records were broken on our Black Monday – biggest one-day fall, biggest volume, more deals on the New York Stock Exchange that day than in the whole of 1950, etc. – that everyone ran out of superlatives, except that no one thought it was particularly superlative. Being the nuclear age John Phelan, chairman of the New York Stock Exchange, described it as 'the closest to meltdown I'd ever want to get'. Believe it or not, when almost every share crashed by 25%, several by 50% and the really wild stocks by even 70%, there were one or two which actually went up. Darren had bought some Scottish Ice Rink shares and was offered £2.50 for them on Black Monday, which he turned down. The next day he was offered £5, which he also turned down. He had a smell for it – why would someone offer him £5 for a share when everything else was crashing round his ears? Finally he was offered £20, which he accepted.

It was a severe test for the new system of dealing whereby the market-makers must show their prices on the screen, which for a beta stock like BBA, a Yorkshire engineering conglomerate, might look like this:

SEAQ COMPETING QUOTES 46609 16.41		
BBA GP		180–81
BZWE	161–164	25 × 25
CIBE	161–164	25 × 25
HOAE	162–165	50 × 50
MGSH	161–164	50 × 50
PADT	160–165	L × L
SAYM	161–164	25 × 25
SBRO	161–164	25 × 25
SVTL	161–164	50 × 50
WARB	160 × 165	L × L

This means that last night's close was 180–181 and that Phillips & Drew (PADT) and Warburg (WARB) are prepared to buy or sell 100,000 shares or over (L × L) at 160 (bid or buy) or 165 (offer or sell). If the broker rings, in theory Warburg and Phillips & Drew must deal in those quantities or those prices.

Top: Dashing for the City through hurricane chaos

Above: Striped shirts in shock. London market-makers watch the Wall Street sell-off on 19 October

DON'T ANSWER THE PHONE

New York, 22 October: a market-maker contemplates his future

What happened on Black Monday was that the Ls, the quantities of 100,000, quickly disappeared from the screens, the spreads widened to say 145-165 (even Shell, which can often be shown with a 2p spread, widened to 20), and while this was happening the market-makers found it exceptionally unrewarding to answer the phones. The investor blamed the broker, the broker blamed the market-maker, the market-maker blamed the new system saying that the screens fell five, even ten minutes behind. In some of the ramped stocks, as we have seen, the jolt was severe. The previous Wednesday you could deal in 250,000, 500,000, even a million with a 2p spread. Suddenly the spread was 4p at a half or even a third of the price and the number, 2,500 shares or maybe 5,000. And that was on a penny stock. On a stock where the price was 300p the spread might be 50p.

Red letter day

Everyone over the age of 40 can remember exactly what they were doing when they heard that President Kennedy had been shot. In the same way every investor will remember what they were doing on 19 October 1987. It was serious, make no mistake. By the middle of Tuesday in New York as the Dow was plunging again – by then it had lost 800 points in less than five trading days – the New York Stock Exchange was in touch with the White House and considering the suspension of trading. At that moment the market rallied and, although it might only be a Dead Cat Bounce, it was at least a bounce and removed the pressure for a moment. If New York had suspended trading the effect on prices in London would have been catastrophic, as that would have been the only escape hatch. The Hong Kong Exchange did suspend trading and that exerted extra pressure elsewhere, especially in Sydney.

Why were the falls so massive? Prices could not keep going up for ever. 'Why

> **PROGRAM TRADING** The automatic buying and selling of shares, options or futures according to computer-based programs.

not?' asked Sid. Good question. No one knows the answer, but they never have before. This does not explain the precipitous plunge. Program trading and portfolio insurance go a long way towards explaining it.

Insuring the portfolio

Portfolio insurance had grown dramatically in popularity in the twelve months before the Crash – the pension fund assets in the USA that were managed in this way had grown from $8.5 billion to $60 billion. In simple terms it meant that by trading in the futures market on the indexes a portfolio could be insured against a fall. Thus you could buy with impunity, which helped to drive the market up, and if it turned you were covered in the futures market, which would just as certainly drive the market down. In theory this is great but the concept has, in retrospect, a rather obvious flaw: if the market is falling, not everyone can be a winner or emerge unscathed. Somebody has to buy what everyone else wants to sell.

Listen to the shoeshine boys

Rockefeller saved his fortune in 1929 by selling out just before the crash. How the hell did he know? Because on the way to his office one morning he stopped to have his shoes cleaned, and the shoeshine boys were discussing stock prices. If shoeshine boys were playing the market and selling, who was left to buy? A shoeshine boy didn't make a lot of dough. In other words there has to be liquidity, and that liquidity was strained to breaking point. There was nothing left to push the market up. This time around it was Sir James Goldsmith who saw the polish on the wall, and sold £150 million worth of shares just before the crash. Jammy.

Someone who's seen it all before

No future in futures

In the week before Black Monday, the portfolio insurers had not been able to sell the stock they wanted to, so by the Monday the pressure was immense. On Black Monday itself, as the insurers sold the futures down below the prices in the market, no one

THE SCREENS
GO RED

**The Crash reverberates
around the world
Right: Tokyo,
26 October
Below: Sydney,
28 October**

would buy the actual stocks when the futures showed they could fall much further, and no one wanted the futures while the portfolio insurers were obvious sellers. The result – a free fall.

There were moments of wry humour. In the States Alan Greenspan, chairman of the Federal Reserve Board, was flying to Dallas to make a speech. The markets were falling as he boarded the plane, so he was greatly relieved when he arrived at Dallas to be told that the Dow Jones was down 'Five Oh Eight' – until he realized the Oh was not a decimal point.

Panic sets in

On Tuesday in New York, in spite of another huge fall in London in response to Wall Street's 500-point drop the previous night, we witnessed the classic Dead Cat Bounce, and the Dow gained 200 points in the first hour. Then the insurers moved in again on the futures and down went the market again, 225 points in two hours. There was real panic now – any further falls (and the futures market was signalling another 300 points) would send many dealers to the wall. The futures market in Chicago stopped trading, apparently believing that the decision to close New York had been taken. As everyone waited, the first sign of a turn came from the little-used Major Market Index in Chicago where there was a rally. New York 'toughed it out'; some corporations helped by announcing they were buying their own stock; and the day finished with a 100-point gain – the largest ever. The immediate crisis was over. The post-mortem began.

Settlement Day

The Stock Exchange operates an account trading system and each account lasts usually two, sometimes three weeks. Any

> **HAMMERED** A stockbroker who cannot meet his obligations is 'hammered'. The term stems from the custom of a Stock Exchange official called a waiter who used to strike the arm of his seat three times, to bring the floor to silence.

transactions made in the account have to be settled on the Monday ten days after the end of the account. So the settlement day for the account including Black Monday was Monday, 2 November. The brokers wanted to know if all their clients would be able to pay. No doubt some investors wondered if their brokers would be able to pay them. After all, in the last bear market, in 1974, seven brokers had been unable to meet their commitments and had been 'hammered'.

FREE FALL

BLOODY ANALYSTS.

deal of confusion about computers in the markets. In London the transmitting of prices and deals is handled by the SEAQ and TOPIC computers, and it is not these that were blamed for the volatility of prices, although there was criticism of whether the new computer systems put in at Big Bang could actually cope.

No – the heavy criticism was of computer or program trading. We have already seen how the portfolio insurers affected activity on Black Monday and Tuesday. Compounding their efforts were the index arbitrageurs. These guys make their supposedly risk-free profits by exploiting anomalies between the underlying prices of stocks and the prices of their futures. These do occasionally get out of line and the arbs, prompted by their computers, move in fast to take advantage before they move back into line.

The three-stage collapse of a market-maker: contemplation ... desolation ...

The investors did not really need to worry unless they were very big punters. There was a Stock Exchange compensation fund which paid up to £250,000 if a member defaulted. The brokers had more worries, and certainly there were slow payers and non-payers. There were also some spectacular losers on the options pitch as well as some big losers on the IG Index, where it is possible to bet at so much a point on the movement of the index. £1,000 a point soon mounts up when the index moves 250 points in a day.

Computers are useful scapegoats

Computers were certainly useful scapegoats, but as Ricky says, 'If you're going to ban computers in stock market trading, why not ban calculators too?' There is a great

The index arbs

On Black Monday the initial sharp fall brought both the portfolio insurers and the index arbs into play. Under normal circumstances these two should provide some sort of balance, with the arbs buying futures and the insurers selling them. But the selling of the futures was so heavy it paid the arbs to sell actual stock. This prompted the insurers to sell more futures, which prompted the arbs to sell more stock, and so on and so on. So yes, the computers and program trades can accentuate trends, but it was ever thus in markets. What makes markets is over-reaction, both up and down. If everyone behaved rationally prices would never move at all, because everyone would agree what the price should be. Markets will have their way, computers or not. When the authorities suspended automatic computer trading after Black Monday the Dow still managed an 8% fall in one day.

Gone to Cabinet

Peter, scared stiff by the Crash, did not do any deals again until March 1988 – and, being Peter, got beautifully caught in a classic suckers' rally. It had happened to an earlier generation of Peters, who, after the Wall Street Crash of autumn 1929, started buying again in the spring when the market had recovered half its fall. All they got for their pains was two years of sliding prices.

So in 1988 Peter bought an April 330 call in GKN. With the GKN price at 334 to 336 he paid 10p for it, or rather £100 for each contract (remember contracts are in thousands). He was looking for a rise in the price to, say, 350 within the next few days, in which case his option would probably have doubled to 20. Instead the market fell, GKN fell faster, and within two weeks the price was 292 and his option had gone to Cabinet.

CABINET If your broker tells you the price of your traded option is Cabinet to 2 it means it will cost you 2 (or 1,000 x 2 in fact) to buy any more. If you want to sell the option you bought with such confidence you will get nothing.

THE SUCKERS' RALLY

... incantation

-8- HIRE AND FIRE

LOADSA CAKE

Let's look at the City back in 1985 as if it were a cake. In the icing on the top were the partners in the broking and jobbing firms. These lucky few received £750 million – it's nice in the icing. But if the cake had such splendid icing it must have had some pretty good marzipan too, and in that layer were the dealers, analysts, and jobbers or market-makers. By late 1985 top gilts dealers were being paid £250,000, more than 25 times the average earnings in industry and ten times the level at which the Labour Party thought everyone was disgustingly rich and should be taxed a lot more. Eurobond dealers would be turning their noses up at £250,000 and looking for £300,000, while the senior executives, former partners or not, would expect to see the magic million on their CV even if, for the moment, it had a half in front

of it. Senior analysts, effectively the people who analyse companies so that their brokers (salesmen) can persuade people to buy shares in the company, would expect to be earning over £100,000 plus the annual bonus, which at this time ranged from 50 to 75%. At Geoffrey Collier's trial, Robert Alexander QC stated that his client would have lost more than £250,000 in salary and fringe benefits – and this for someone who was so bright he seemed to lose more often than not, even when he had inside information.

What about the rest of the cake? Well, of course that wasn't quite as tasty, but even so rates were dragged up and there was loadsa money to be found in ordinary clerical jobs for the fruits, and the nuts were paid probably twice as well as elsewhere.

OK, this is it. What do those lucky bastards get paid in 1988?

A mere bagatelle

Let's start somewhere near the top. Forty-two-year-old Christopher Heath, who runs the Far East share dealing operation for Baring Brothers, was paid £2.5 million in 1987. That's £50,000 a week. In other words he was paid five times as much in a week as most nurses got paid in a year, and since the '88 Budget reduced the top tax whack to 40%, that means he takes home £1,500,000 a year. Chancellor Lawson handed him a rise of half a million quid. In the wrong hands that's the sort of thing that could give the City a bad name.

In fact it is a mere bagatelle compared with some New York salaries. On the Street, as Tel would put it, Michel David-

Weill, a senior partner of Lazard Freres, was paid $125 million in 1987, while the famous George Soros of money managers Soros Management paid himself $100 million. (Next time you see him, ask George about the Dead Cat Bounce. He saw the Crash coming, though he thought it would start in Tokyo, and he bought when the cat bounced on the Wednesday after the Crash, before it plunged again.) Richard Dennis of C&D Commodities and Michael Mikken of Drexel, Burnham & Lambert had to struggle by on a paltry $80 million.

Operating in a world market

What this does highlight is that the City has finally realized that it is operating in a world market and that salaries will be forced up to international levels, especially for the best people.

The clearing banks – Lloyds, NatWest, Midland, Barclays – must be having some difficulty convincing the managers on the commercial side and in the high street that their £25,000 is an adequate reward when their brothers on the securities side in the City are earning over £100,000, and while they are doing it they are making some spectacular losses. NatWest reported in 1987 that out of 94,000 employees there were fewer than 90 earning over £50,000 and only eight were paid over £100,000 – keep working for those Americans, Charlotte. Lloyds was even more niggardly; apart from two directors only one employee was paid more than £100,000.

Seriously well paid

In order to be a seriously well-paid bank employee it obviously helps to be international – Hervé de Carmoy, who was head of Midland Bank's global banking operations, was paid £748,458 in 1987 (nearly four times as much as the chairman and CEO, Sir Kit McMahon), while his German pal Ernst Brutsche took away over £625,000 as boss of the Midland's investment banking and treasury operations. Only two years earlier,

$2.5 MILLION A WEEK

Sunday Times, **24 January 1988**

BUSINESS FOCUS

● **How far is your annual salary from £270,000? That is now the average pay of Britain's 100 highest-paid company directors. Performance-related schemes have helped push the earnings of top executives to these new heights, but will their wage packets go back to basics if times turn sour?**

PHILIP BERESFORD and JUDI BEVAN report

BRITAIN's highest paid businessman makes £48,000. Every week.

For Christopher Heath, that adds up to £2.5m a year.

But the 41-year-old managing director of Baring Securities, part of the exclusive Baring Brothers Bank, has little chance to spend the money on his Kensington house or indulge his passion for racehorses. He is on the road six months of the year, mainly in Tokyo, dealing in the Japanese stock market for his clients.

This demanding life-style is typical of the top British executives who in the Thatcher years are rediscovering the rewards as well as the satisfaction of hard work.

Heath's earnings are a [...] sum beside the average [...] wage of £10,000, and a [...] way ahead of some of the [...] try's best known busi[...]men.

[...] list of the 100 highest [...] directors in Britain shows [...] a handful now earning an [...] salary of more than [...] The average for the top [...] about £270,000. [...] financiers and retailers [...]come the stars in the [...]

worked until four in the morning for three nights running during the recent launch of the Next Directory.

"I simply won't give in on a project until I know it's right," he says.

Three years ago, BOC group's Dick Giordano was front page news when he became the first executive to break the £750,000 barrier. Yet when Lord Hanson's salary nearly tripled to over £1.2m at the end of last year, there was barely a ripple of complaint.

"More remuneration packages for senior executives are being set with fairly tough business targets," says John Gilbert, director of financial services consulting at Hay Management Consultants.

If performance has become the principle criterion, measuring it has become easier. Swathes of middle managers have disappeared from companies, leaving few nooks to shelter the non-performers.

"Major organisations are now leaner and tougher. There has been a general devolution of accountability down the organisation so managers have three or four key objectives which they know they have to [...] says.

The comforts of home: Christopher Heath takes time out from his commuting schedule to Tokyo

THE TOP SALARY PACKETS

	Name	Company	Salary £000	Salary rise, %	Profits rise, %
1	Christopher Heath	Baring	2,500		
2	Sir Ralph Halpern	Burton	1,390	35	23
3	Lord Hanson	Hanson	1,263	286	60
4	Michael Slade	Helical Bar	1,106		
5	P Stormonth-Darling	Warburg	1,051		
6	Gerald Ronson	Heron	831	93	26
7	Richard Giordano	BOC	782	1	23
8	Tiny Rowland	Lonrho	476	21	4
9	Ephraim Margulies	Berisford, S&W	472	210	180
10	Unidentified	Assoc Newspapers	393	95	10
11	Sir John Harvey-Jones	ICI	383	26	11
12	George Mallinckrodt	Schroder	384	11	
13	Robert Bauman	Beecham	366		15
14	Lloyd Bensen	Ultramar	348	17	−73
15	B Christopher	BSR	332	−13	250
16	Peter Balfour	R Bank of Scotland	327	146	7
17	Philip Birch	Ward White	317	41	59
18	Richard Haxwell	Norton Opax	314	127	223
19	John Craven	Morgan Grenfel	310		
20	Paul Girolami	Glaxo	309	27	22
21	Bernard Matthews	Bernard Matthews	306	33	17
22	Unidentified	Sedgwick	303	107	9
23	Sir Peter Walters	BP	301	15	−72
24	Unidentified	Abaco	300		400
25	Maurice Saatchi	Saatchi & Saatchi	298	32	71
26	Sir D Holden-Brown	Allied-Lyons	293	101	2
27	Geoffrey Mulcahy	Woolworth	291	101	
28	Lord Rayner	Marks & Spencer	287	32	
29	J Haythornthwaite	Scapa Group	285	5	
30	Anthony Tennant	Guinness	283		
31	George Davies	Next	283	123	
32	James White	Bunzl	281	46	
33	Unidentified	Cater Allen	280	−11	
34	Peter Holmes	Shell Transport	260	34	
35	Sir Owen Green	BTR	260	32	
36	Arthur Walsh	STC	257	11	1
37	James Gulliver	Argyll	252	16	
38	Alan Weltz	London Int	252	3	
39	Rudolph Agnew	Cons Gold	244	12	
40	Sir Eric Sharp	Cable & Wireless	238	31	
41	Eric Parker	Trafalgar House	236	5	
42	Alfred Sheppard	Wellcome	236	44	
43	Unidentified	Anschacher, Henry	235	48	
44	Roy Pettitt	Minet	234	29	2
45	Neil Shaw	Tate & Lyle	232	8	
46	Sir R Crichton-Brown	Rothmans	230	0	
47	Michael Hawkes	Kleinwort Benson	228	−5	
48		Marley	225	110	
49		Plessey	225	3	

THE BRIGHT YOUNG THINGS

in 1985, the highest-paid Midland director earned a paltry £120,000. In 1986, after Midland had absorbed Greenwells, there were seven earning more than £120,000, with the highest at £188,840. By early 1988 Greenwells' equity business no longer existed.

In the spring of 1988 Barclays reported that 17 of its directors in the BZW subsidiary, which lost £13.2 million, were paid over £100,000, two of them over £190,000.

The chairman, John Quinton, was earning £220,000.

There is no question that Big Bang brought a sharp escalation in salaries. Of course, the hours of work have changed. A few years ago the gilt-edged brokers and jobbers would start at 10 as the market opened, though there would be the odd conference at 9.30. The market closed at 3.30 and there might be a bit of kerb trading until 5. Now the market opens at 9 and there is always a conference at 8. Trading does not stop when the London market closes, but goes on with the USA until 9 p.m.

The ripple effect of high salaries for the big players means higher if not high salaries for everyone else. In the big-volume days of 1987 nearly all the stockbrokers got way behind in their back, i.e. settlement, offices. The good admin. guys were suddenly in demand and one of the best, Rab Harley, was poached from Wood Mackenzie with the offer of a £200,000 salary. By August 1987 Brook Street Bureau were placing school leavers with good shorthand typing at £7,000 and telling them that in a year or so they would be earning £15,000 – 20,000.

A piddling £55,000

The insanity of '85 and '86 has in some areas led to falls in rates of pay where the demand has exceeded the supply. By early '88 headhunters were still handling Eurobond dealers, but if they had five years' experience they could no longer demand – and get – £150,000. 'I can't believe it,' said one fresh-faced dealer in his twenties. 'They only offered me a piddling £55,000. Bloody nerve.' If they only had two years' experience, pre-Crash levels of £60,000 had plunged to £20,000. And it was not only in the Eurobond area. Senior gilt-edged salesmen had also lost the six-figure cachet, plunging from £150,000 to £65,000.

The milk round

In the new meritocracy graduates, never mind the school, are wanted, and by 1987 the top City houses were on the milk round looking for the best. The Japanese Nomura were offering starting salaries of £16,000, Midland Montagu were more modest at £12,500, Schroder's were at £13,500, while the good old Americans Credit Suisse First Boston were punting at £17,500. Twenty years ago graduates were OK but not sought after, and their starting salaries were under £1,000 – about what a London secretary made.

Merchant banks have 74%, stockbrokers 41%, clearing banks 29% and foreign banks 51% of their new entrants coming from Camford. Whereas in the sixties these Bright Young Things would have gone into publishing, journalism, television or advertising, now Charlotte and her friends make tracks for the City. Starting salaries of up to £25,000 combined with perks like cheap mortgages have, not surprisingly, considerable appeal to final-year students. Traditional Oxbridge recruiters like the Civil Service are having difficulty obtaining the highest quality of Administrative trainee, who starts at a paltry £11,000, because of the pull of the Porsche lifestyle. They are even losing to the City serious numbers of the young trainees they've taken on.

Other traditionally popular homes for new graduates have even less appeal on the financial front. Never mind the Porsche – a starting salary of £6,000-7,000 won't even support a second-hand 2CV for the budding publisher with an Oxbridge first in English. A management trainee in industry or retailing – Mars or Marks & Spencer, say – will go in on £9,000-9,500. Computer programming, once the first port of call for third-year students with the get-rich quick

GET OFF THE PREMISES

urge when prospective employers came on the university milk round, has fallen behind and only offers newcomers about £10,000. Advertising and PR, often quoted as big payers, start surprisingly low at £11,000-ish – but there are great prospects if you're really bright. Getting nearer the level of City pay cheques are the management consultants, who offer about £18,000 to graduate trainees, but they're very choosy – they wouldn't have taken Charlotte. But who needs to work for a management consultant when by 27 you can get £100,000 in the City?

Our degree-less market-maker Tel gets a reasonable stack from his bank – £65,000 plus car, plus bonus which in a normal year would be 50–60%, plus BUPA, plus hefty pension contribution, plus mortgage subsidy, plus generous expense allowance. He's happy with this and has in fact turned down higher offers from elsewhere.

Sacked over the tannoy

In '85 and '86 it was all hire, and at rapidly increasing rates. In '87 and '88 the fire came in and sometimes more like a machine gun than a rocket. After the Crash no one in the City could seriously expect to feel utterly secure in his or her job. As the Americans led the bidding up they seemed to lack a certain subtlety in letting people down. One US bank even summoned those it was sacking one by one over the public address system. Another, which had only recently taken on 20 graduate trainees and had gone to great lengths to recruit those of the highest calibre, suddenly made the following announcement over the public address system, 'Will all graduate trainees clear their desks and report to personnel.' Some of those graduates are eventually going to get to the top and they are not likely to forget the bank that did that to them.

Another American hatchet man was sent from New York and asked for all personnel records which itemized salaries against earnings for the company. He fired the lowest earners and then came to a group who seemed to earn nothing at all. They were off the premises double quick, and not till Friday was it discovered that he had sacked all the messengers. A dealer at Goldman Sachs returned from holiday and only realized he had been sacked when he saw that on his VDU his initials, which flash when he is wanted on the phone, had been removed. At another US securities house in London, brokers had to wait for the new telephone directory to be issued: if you were in it, fine; if not, not.

Getting your own back

The tendency of most firms is to get

sacked employees off the premises immediately. In some cases they have been escorted off, which prevents any ugly scenes. It also prevents any disgruntled dealer writing some ridiculous options which could cost the company millions (although you don't need to be sacked to accomplish that at some firms). Champagne Charlie had now become Redundant Reggie and he didn't like it a bit. One Reggie drove his company Porsche up to the front doors of the bank, put the alarm on and threw the keys down a drain. That just caused the bank some embarrassment, but another Reggie put in a call which lasted all weekend to the Los Angeles speaking clock.

Employers were taking no more chances after that story. The next lot to go were asked for their security passes as they arrived one morning. Then the open-mouthed employees were told, 'We're sorry, you don't work here any more.' Perhaps the most damaging – and, of course, dangerous – act of revenge was nearly perpetrated in March '88 when one fired employee piled all his papers on the floor in the middle of the dealing room. His bemused colleagues only realized at the last minute that this was a prelude to another sort of firing which would have set off all the sprinkler systems, ruining millions of pounds' worth of equipment.

County NatWest fired 165 employees in February 1988 when the Scot John Chiene came in with Wood Mackenzie. That blood-letting was referred to as 'The Chiene Saw Massacre.' Never to be out-done, Chiene replied, 'In choosing who was to stay we wanted the best people. It doesn't matter if they wore tartan trews or not.' It was rumoured that some of the 165 were not impressed and smashed their screens, caus-ing £150,000 of damage – cheap compared with the rogue deals they might have done

if they had kept the screens working.

Of course there was nothing personal about the sackings. The testimonials and references were glowing. 'I can't recom-mend Georgina too highly'; 'James was fired with enthusiasm'.

Constructive dismissal

Getting the boot isn't always a disaster. If you've been around long enough you can negotiate a reasonable exit. One ousted chairman actually had his salary increased when he stopped being chairman and became a consultant instead. It went up from £115,000 a year to £127,000. He also organized the continued use of his chauffeur-driven company car, plus BUPA and his business travel expenses. He enjoys a further £40,000 in lieu of office and ancillary services, plus four Centre Court tickets for the Wimbledon finals and four tickets for each booking period at Covent Garden. And he receives £24,000 a year to cover luncheon expenses for himself and his guests. Assuming he will take four weeks' holiday a year that leaves £100 a day every working day of the week for lunch.

-9- A DAY IN THE FAST LANE

Dawn raiders

The City has always been a jungle, but with the Thatcher Revolution the variety of species attracted to this area has dramatically increased. They may be fighting for survival each working day but at least they can retreat from the jungle for some leisure ` – and sleep. Both are at a premium.

A few City workers actually live in the place, the Barbican for example or the new Docklands yuppie compounds, but the majority commute from all points of the compass – you may have to work in a jungle, but you don't have to spend all your free time there as well. Half a million people flow into the City each morning and flow out again each evening by train, tube, car, motorbike, bicycle, foot and helicopter: how does the day break for our rock pool inhabitants?

Charles, our Old Carthusian, and part of the ever diminishing breed of City Gent, spent his early married days in Oakley Street. Once his children were born the Sloane need for country air and space sent him out to Hampshire, where the combina-

London Bridge 8 a.m.

tion of a cheap mortgage from his employers and a private income bought him an agreeable period house in an attractive village near Basingstoke. Little did he realize how little time he would have to enjoy it.

His alarm goes off at 5.45 and, with his wife still asleep, he dresses quickly in his Savile Row suit, New & Lingwood shirt and Church's shoes (NB no flashy socks). Quickly he snatches a bite to eat, occasionally remembering the days of eggs and bacon, before driving his Maxi to the station – the Volvo Estate remains firmly at home to ferry children and dogs. Charles buys his *FT* and *Times* but can hardly keep his eyes open to read them. The only disturbance to his peace is the irritating warbling of the portable phones that some of his many younger companions on the 6.30 are using. For them the day is already underway. At 7.30 Charles arrives at Waterloo and jostles with the crowds on 'the drain' direct through to Bank.

Arise the Earl of Essex

While Charles is struggling out of bed, Darren is stirring in his modern detached house at Leigh-on-Sea, near Southend. He gropes his way to the en-suite bathroom and thankfully his Jacuzzi brings him quickly to life. There is more spring to his step by the time he moves on to his walk-in cupboard to choose either his Armani or Versace suit, monogrammed shirt and silk tie from Tie Rack – he likes to buy ties from there as he made money on the flotation. He splashes on copious amounts of Ralph Lauren 'Polo'. Having seen *Wall Street* the bright red braces and slicked-back hair provide the finishing touches. His gold bracelet stayed on him all night, but he grabs his gold Rolex before kissing Tracey goodbye.

Checking his hair in the floor-to-ceiling

mirror behind the bed, he makes a dash downstairs and into the car. With one hand on the steering wheel, another pushing Whitney Houston into the six-speaker CD player, a peanut butter sandwich clenched between his teeth, Darren's Porsche 924S is revved into action. Everyone in the road may have been woken up, but at least Darren catches his train to Liverpool Street.

Cobham behind closed doors

D'Arcy, if he is at home – and he spends quite a few nights at his flat in Knightsbridge – is woken by Radio 4 at 6 a.m. He lives in a large 'Surrey Mansion' with two acres of beautifully manicured garden in Cobham. He bought the house after a successful takeover in the late seventies, causing gossip among his friends by the sudden display of wealth.

The au-pair girl, Nicole, only too aware of what d'Arcy's wife is up to during the day – and a pretty shrewd idea of d'Arcy's

Brokers breakfast as trading begins

Go-getters' ghetto: Cascades in the Docklands

double life – is perfectly happy to add fuel to the fire by being up with d'Arcy to prepare his orange juice and toast. She has made sure that his handmade shirts from Turnbull & Asser are exquisitely ironed and while he straightens his Vincents tie – reminding him of his fitter days as an Oxford cricket blue – a few flirtatious remarks are exchanged. Leaving the house in his 7-series BMW, he manages to drive the 20-mile journey in the hour.

Enjoy it while it lasts

Charlotte owns a small house in Fulham, catching the tube from Parsons Green at 7, but as it is so unbearably hot and crowded she has taken out an option on a flat at Cascades in Docklands. It will also mean she can stay in bed longer – if it is her own bed. Although highly paid, she is not over-extended in her work and she is determined to enjoy the good life while it lasts. Char-

lotte may not, in the final analysis, make any waves in the market, but those that know her will appreciate her style – La Perla underwear, Fogel stockings, Calvin Klein suit and Maud Frizon shoes.

So the four join the other players, all with their own pattern of existence – and don't forget those people at the Metal Exchange and LIFFE. For all it is a scramble to meet the early morning start in the office – on a quiet day a quick breakfast at the desk can ease you in, but for most the rush is immediate, with a long wait for lunch.

Out to Lunch

In the golden olden days before Big Bang the theory and practice of lunch occupied a significant part of people's time and mentality. Those were the leisurely days of epic lunches at Whites or the Savoy, consisting of the full trooping the colour of traditional English gastronomy: soup, fish, roast, savoury, pudding and cheese, accompanied by oceans of claret and concluded with port, brandy and cigars. Return to the office was delayed until 4, if not actually omitted. The participants all felt sated and happy in the knowledge that they had participated in an ancient rite. The actual amount of business concluded was minimal, but the ritual giving and consuming of food and drink cemented the network of personal contacts by which the old City operated.

Even on ordinary days lunch was a solid two-hour affair in the City's numberless dark brown Dickensian chophouses (like the George and Vulture) and public houses (like the Jamaica), with large amounts of serious drinking. These places still exist, but the City lunch has been dramatically transformed. Firms realized that if they were paying someone a telephone number salary to play an upmarket version of Space Invaders on a video screen, the essential hair-trigger responses and ability to conjure money out of the fine differences between numbers was unlikely to be improved by marinading them in two bottles of St Emilion between 1 and 3. And the markets were open all day – what was their man doing wasting his substance when he could be trading?

Daytime drinking was discouraged. The white-wine-and-fizzy-water 'Spritzer' expanded its appeal from nervous secretaries and commended itself to large men clothed in Gieves & Hawkes' best. Perrier, Badoit and other waters became common and unremarkable choices as beverages. Wine bars mutated from oak-panelled, all-male claret and roast beef sandwich dispensaries like El Vino's to high-tech quiche-nibblers' haunts like Corney & Barrow in Moorgate.

The £5 Sandwich

Going all out for lunch was no longer tolerated, and this stimulated the rise of the Designer Sandwich. Ghastly old caffs which slapped processed cheese slices on the Sunblest with a hint of Stork disappeared, and were replaced by super-efficient emporia like Birleys (started by the son of the owner of Annabels nightclub), where smartly packaged sandwiches began to contain expensive things like pastrami and gravlax in big portions in the American style. Sandwich bars now compete in the City to deliver exotic variants on something between two (or sometimes three) slices of bread. 'Avocado, stone-crab and mango on rye? Pas de problème.' 'Prawn, lychee, anchovy and mayonnaise in a bagel? With you in twenty minutes, squire.' Thus, a screen jockey can satisfy the inner man without raising his eyes from the VDU. It doesn't come cheap, though. The Day of the

£5 Sandwich has arrived.

Old Lunch can still be found in certain places: many firms employ young Sloane Rangers to cook lunch for the directors. The job has become one of the stations of the cross for Carolines and Sophies as they fill in time before marriage, along with being a

Refreshing the parts the computers cannot reach: City lunch break

Keeping your bottle as the day wears on

traditional establishments, like Sweeting's Fish Restaurant where the menu concludes with bread-and-butter pudding, treacle tart and jam roly-poly.

New Lunch happens in glamorous designer hangouts like Rouxl Britannia, Coates Café or the Corney & Barrow complex in Moorgate. Slickers may drink less but they pay much more for what they do drink – and they're getting knowledge-able. They take the Christie's wine course (£100 for eight evening guided tastings) to learn the basics, and buy by the case using Robert Parker's indispensable *Wine Buyer's Guide*. All the restaurants have serious wine lists and serious food. Since semi-oblivion is no longer the point of lunch, City types now actually notice what they eat: chic nouvelle dishes in colourful puddles, grilled chèvre, monkfish, red mullet, smoked sturgeon, swordfish, walnut oil salads. The City's most impressive food at most impressive prices comes at Roux brothers' pride and joy, the directors' dining room downstairs at Le Poulbot (possibly losing its touch in the last year, though).

Keep out the natives

The arrival of our friends from Tokyo in the market caused a sharp rise in the number of Japanese bars and restaurants. They are all very, very expensive, partly to keep out the natives (us), and partly because the raw materials for dishes like sushi and sashimi need to be as fresh as possible, otherwise you die. The staff are highly skilled and won-drous to behold – the chef cooks everything with exquisite artistry in front of you and serves up delicious bite-sized morsels of steak and prawn. The Japanese prefer to keep themselves to themselves and they use these establishments as clubs. Behind the bar at Hana Gurama and Ginnan you will find a shelf covered with bottles of Scotch in

chalet girl in Verbier, working on the front desk at Christie's, and enduring the Cordon Bleu course. The girls provide items from the undemanding Sloane school of cookery: smoked salmon, oysters, boeuf en croute, salmon steaks, Elizabeth David's ubiquitous but peerless chocolate mousse, Stilton. The nursery food element is still strong in the

DESPERATELY SEEKING SUSHI

Nips for the Japs: personal whisky bottles behind the bar

varying stages of emptiness. Each has a label in Japanese identifying its owner, who will come in and have a drink from his own bottle. Karaoke bars have recently arrived in London, strictly for the Japanese diaspora; who else would pay lots of money for the privilege of singing along with a jukebox but the people who pay fortunes for handsculpted raw tuna. Very inscrutable.

Banking on bubbly

Although exact figures are hard to come by, it is almost certainly the case that London bankers and brokers are the biggest per capita consumers of champagne in the world. They get through more than a million bottles every year – around a fifteenth of Britain's total consumption – and that's just working-time drinking. Bol-

linger and Veuve Clicquot are the City's traditional favourites, but Darren and his pals are partial to pink champagne and the

Lunchtime sanctuary for the screen-shocked: St Mary Woolnoth

junior fund manager, with one of her team's salesmen, or several of them with a representative of one of the major retailers. If there is no business lunch she'll meet her girlfriends in a Balls Bros wine bar, or in the Bottlescrue on Holborn Viaduct.

Lunch used to be pretty relaxed time-wise, but lately it has been suggested that people should be back in the office for Wall Street's opening. This is 1.30 our time, although the 'grey' market will have been operating all morning. All the important US economic figures (like the trade deficit) are also announced at 1.30 our time. These can have dramatic effects on currency and bond markets, here as well as in the States. So, on those days, it's a designer sandwich at the screen.

Pass the Pigs

For some an hour spent at a gym hall providing physical exercise, cards and drinking, all under the same roof, is what is needed at lunchtime. And younger Slickers do enjoy playing games. The great success of the past few years, Trivial Pursuit, is not the great hit you might imagine in the City. That's because the great majority of players have little or no general knowledge and they tend to lose, which is not an experience they enjoy. Pass the Pigs, a sort of porcine dice game, is far more popular as it's readily portable and you can bet on it.

For a few none of these outlets is what they want and the strain of a morning's work is better dealt with by some time spent at St Mary Woolnoth. Here there is time to relax. And it is certainly preferable to dabbling in drugs.

The Powder Room

The Powder Room has taken on a whole new meaning in the City, and it doesn't refer to the invasion by the Monstrous

extremely expensive Louis Roederer Cristal (Joan Collins' favourite tipple in *Dynasty*). Darren celebrated his staging of Sock Shop at the Greenhouse (just beside LIFFE) with three bottles of Krug '59 at £53.90 each.

Lunch for Charlotte might involve entertaining an institutional client, probably a

Regiment. Nor does Coke necessarily mean the tasty and nutritious product canned by that nice company in Atlanta, Ga.

Cocaine is the City's illegal drug of choice (alcohol still tops the all-drug hit-parade). It's expensive – but who cares if you're making £100K? – it's glamorous – models, rock stars and Hollywood producers use it – and it's got a good image. It sharpens your reflexes for your high-pressure job and makes you feel much better about yourself and life – unlike other stuff which will leave you talking to plants or taking three hours to find the door. Coke addicts don't seem to wind up squalidly OD'd in public lavatories; even being a casualty has class. The less agreeable symptoms – manic depression, raging paranoia, insomnia – don't seem to register, probably because this is the natural state for foreign exchange traders.

Cocaine is now a bigger threat than alcohol to efficient working in the City. Whereas in the old days youngsters would speak in hushed and reverent terms of a 'three-bottle-a-day man', more of them than you might think are having to set aside increasingly substantial proportions of their income to sustain their addiction. It has been estimated that as many as 80% of London's cokeheads work in the City. Testing for drugs has arrived in Wall Street, but has yet to make it across the Atlantic. The City of London police take little action against coke dealing in the City; the Metropolitan force operates against drugs on a macro level.

The coke blip panic

Firms are aware of the dangers: here is a possible scenario. Wednesday afternoon, 15.34. Shrivelled eyeballs try to outstare screens. Suddenly Amalgamated Consolidated International adds 214% to its share price, which has remained relatively static since the company was founded in 1892. Momentary panic breaks out, which is calmed when the rogue price is found to have been caused by a coke blip. Some young man has misjudged the amount of his post-prandial snort and has lost his company £100K in as many seconds. Another briefcase, another hall.

Santa operates a delivery service. Instead of the hassle of haggling for drugs in the street, the head brigade run accounts with dealers who deliver your toot of God's dandruff person to person, using unsuspecting legitimate courier services. All major credit cards accepted. The fashion spread from the New York Stock Exchange, where discreet cards are passed around which bear only a telephone number and the words 'We Deliver'. Darren used to be friendly with the company's agent (or pusher, in actual fact) until he pushed his luck a little too far one day. Darren is not what one might call a moralist; he has simply seen what has happened to the snorters and has no wish to board a sinking ship.

A TOOT OF GOD'S DANDRUFF

NO DAYLIGHT FOR CHARLES

Closing Time

The working day draws to a close – at least in London. The New York Exchange goes on until 9.30 and then Tokyo opens after that. Money doesn't sleep and some continue chasing it round the world throughout the night. For most, however, 6.30 is quitting time.

Charles can remember the days when he would leave at 5 o'clock and on Fridays at 4.30. Now everyone still seems to be on the

Tips and tipples at the end of the day: Jamaica Wine House

phone at 5.30, even 6 o'clock, so he feels he'd better hang around too. Surely he can leave at 6.30. Yes. Back on 'the drain', catch the 7 o'clock from Waterloo, with a chat or snooze en route. Oh God, someone's portable phone is warbling again, but at least the chat with Sonya is more fun to overhear than the early morning business calls.

For six months of the year Charles sees no daylight for five days each week, except for a brief snatch at lunchtime – at least he is luckier than some who aren't even allowed to leave their building during the day. He now envies his friends who stayed in London and live in Holland Park, but there is no way that Fiona would contemplate relinquishing her cosy existence. Her days are wonderful and there is so much for her to chatter about over dinner that she doesn't even realize that for the last year Charles has never talked about the office. He's a good listener but certainly not the life and soul of the Friday night dinner party.

The Dynasty siren from Leigh-on-Sea

Tracey, Darren's girlfriend, works as a hairdresser. They met at school. Every Tuesday and Friday she comes up to town in a minicab, dressed like a *Dynasty* siren with her hair done specially by her mate Sharon at their salon. She meets Darren at Corney & Barrow, where he is having a quick Grolsch, having closed his book at 6.30. Tuesdays they will go on to a show (Lloyd Webber's *Phantom of the Opera* was fantastic) and Fridays they bop till they drop at Stringfellows, where they call the owner Pete. Tracey reads *Blitz*, and will occasionally persuade Darren to try out other nightclubs, as long as they have been written about in magazines.

D'Arcy is constantly involved in takeovers and many of his evenings are

EVENING STARS

**Bubbly conversation at
Corney & Barrow**

genuinely taken up with meetings to discuss strategy, or entertaining clients. Others are taken up with entertaining Caroline, an independent 35-year-old who is bright enough to reflect d'Arcy's view of himself in return for dinner at Le Suquet and a drink at Annabels afterwards. Even later, at 3 a.m. say, he might be amending legal documents or arranging huge money transfers. The final details of takeovers tend to be worked out exhaustingly and exhaustively in the small hours. He may move between Cobham and Knightsbridge during the week, but d'Arcy does share one interest with his wife Anne – sailing – and all their summer weekends are spent at Bembridge.

High performance in bed

Charlotte has no constraints on her time in the evening and with her style she can pick and choose the men she wants to spend the evening with. If it is someone else from the City – at least they talk the same language – she has to make sure she sets the right pace. Not too much alcohol and not too long a meal at Bibendum – her current favourite eating place – otherwise he will be asleep before his head hits the pillow. In this high-performance world you don't get into Charlotte's bed just for a drunken five-minute bounce.

-10- CRUCIAL ACCESSORIES

DEALERS' WHEELS

True Brit

Cars are symbols of how we view ourselves. Only the dreamers and the utterly self-assured are oblivious of the car they drive. Jeffrey Archer maintained he did not know what car he drove but somehow it still had the number plate ANY 1. In the City, cars are used to tell the world what you want them to know about you. You may get it wrong, of course – for example, Rolls Royces are unbelievably naff. Even the firm itself admits that most of their output is bought by self-made men in thrall to the illusion that they are buying 'the best car in the world'. The Bentley is for the same person who doesn't want a chauffeur.

Chairmen of leading merchant banks do not have Rolls or Bentleys and snigger at those who do. They slide gracefully into their new chauffeur-driven Jaguars at 6.30

p.m. and pick up the telephone. Since the wonderful Sir John Egan revived Jaguar, it is now not only patriotic to have a Jaguar, but also sensible. At the price, it is easily the best car in the world. There has been talk in the City that they are too cheap. People would like to pay more.

The Range Rover would not be used by anyone who wanted to be serious in the City. It has never seen a field in its life, but it shows everyone that the owner does not mind buying petrol for a machine that does 10 miles to the gallon picking up dry-cleaning in Pont Street.

Porsche

Among the younger set the Porsche is the ultimate status symbol, but as with cars in general, there is a definite pecking order. The 959 and the 911 Sport Turbo can't be regarded as day-to-day transport, so top of the pops is the 928S. This, complete with all the sprack, will be driven by Darren's friend Tel from Romford, who has done pheno-menally well as a market-maker.

The bottom-of-the-range Porsche, the ludicrously over-priced £21,000 924S, is bought by young stockbrokers and market-makers in their early twenties, and insured third party only. They can talk about them incessantly and boringly, and the friends of one City Slicker were recently forced to advertise his Porsche in the *Evening Standard* for £5,000 less than its market value in order to shut him up. They reasoned that so many people would ring up about the car he would chat about it to his heart's content.

ALL THE SPRACK

Charlotte's had a car allowance as part of her perks since she was 24, though as a junior research analyst she could hardly have warranted one. Nevertheless, she was rather disappointed because, at first, it was so meagre that it only enabled her to buy a Peugeot 205 GTI. Now she's got the regulation red Porsche 944 she's feeling a whole lot better.

BMW

BMW, makers of the 'ultimate driving machine', have had an extraordinary triumph as the standard off-the-peg banker-mobile. What can it be? What has made this machine, perfectly designed for cruising at 110 m.p.h. down autobahns, the first choice for crawling in second gear from Clapham to the City in the rush hour? Is it the way only another BMW driver can tell the different models apart without looking at the numbers written on them? Is it the image of German technical efficiency? Or is it because it shows that you are a no-nonsense, let's-get-on-with-it, is-the-market-up-or-down type? Whatever it is there are a lot of them around – not least because BMW have diluted the bottom of the market with their under-powered 3 series. They seem to be losing their appeal recently, possibly because second-hand models have proved extremely popular with members of the West Indian community in Brixton. Telephones are essential. Any colour as long as it's black.

Hot Hatches

Golf GTIs, Escort XR3is and Peugeot 205 GTIs are bought by the Essex Boys who are still living at home giving Mum £20 towards the housekeeping (which is why Charlotte was so upset – that Peugeot did nothing for her image). Darren used to drive an XR3i but has recently replaced it with a Porsche 924S loaded with sprack: carphone (natch), air conditioning (or fridge, as he prefers to call it, and which is about as useful in England as a cashmere sweater in Singapore) and six-speaker CD player.

TWO-PIECE TIPS

Dress for Success

If you're not wearing a suit in the City, you're invisible. If you're not in a suit you must be a bike-boy or delivering sandwiches. And you can't just wear any old suit, it must be:

1) wool (if it's polyester you are a low-grade operative in the back office)

2) black, grey or blue – it is not even conceivable that you could wear brown or green and still have your job when the markets close

3) plain, pinstripe, chalk stripe, just possibly Prince of Wales check – everything else is nowhere

4) double-breasted or single-breasted: currently a 50-50 split. The higher the echelon the more double-breasteds there are. (In Wall Street, however, double-breasted suits are considered rather low-rent.)

Traditional suits are made to measure from all the Savile Row tailors – Huntsman, Gieves & Hawkes etc. – and cost a fortune. Young traditionals get their charcoal-grey suits at Hackett in Parsons Green (£250 or so each) or in Harrods sale.

In the days before Big Bang, when you actually had to physically get on the dealing floor at the Stock Exchange, any infringement of this strict dress code would be punished by debagging (if your tie was considered inappropriate, pretty soon someone would cut it in two with a pair of scissors). Nowadays, unsuitable clothes merely carry the penalty that no one is able to hear what you are saying, and that your job is being advertised.

For some, screaming silk linings

Inside these strict rules, however, you can play several small variations to express your individuality. Some brokers are keen on

Wall Street in Cheapside

coloured silk linings, the more screaming the better. Turn-ups probably indicate a transatlantic influence: Preppies in New York are very keen on them, London only moderately. Waistcoats are rare.

A few fashion trends are, however, not unknown in the City, especially among the younger bloods. A recent craze was armbands, but since the sartorial stereotype they represent was written rather too large in *Wall Street*, fewer Slickers are interested in living up to it and armbands are now on their way out. Braces, worn with high-backed trousers (leather loops essential, clip-ons definitely out) are another fashion fad. The current fashion is the detachable shirt collar – the rediscovery of tradition is the key to City trendsetting.

For others, nothing too flamboyant

There are only pure cotton, striped or white shirts in the City. They come from New & Lingwood, Harvie & Hudson, Turnbull & Asser and Thomas Pink. New York-influenced types will have Brooks Bros button-down collars. Grandees will have them made to measure.

The double cuffs are held together with gold or silver double-sided cufflinks or those little pastel knotted balls of silk thread. Nothing too flamboyant. Ties have become more sophisticated in the last five years. Once upon a time wearing anything other than a polka-dot or a regimental tie (*not* an old school tie) would have ended your career. Now only old duffers wear regimental ties, and Young Turks keep a harem of expensive and exotic neckwear. Well, not too exotic, but they might well take a step beyond Hermès, maybe even Scott Crolla. They are always silk. (Tie Rack do immense business in the City because clean-

ing silk ties is so difficult and expensive; might as well buy a new one.)

Shoes are black Oxfords or black brogues. Preppies will try a pair of tassel loafers occasionally, but slip-ons are generally too casual for any except Darren and his chums. The real City aristocrat will have them made to measure at Trickers in

Where to buy your uniform: New & Lingwood

LABEL POWER

Jermyn Street or Lobbs in St James's Street. Like so many other peripheral services attracted by abundant City cash, there are shoe-shining entrepreneurs (often public schoolchildren in their vacations) doing the rounds of the wine bars and offices to ensure that your uppers can reflect your winner's smile.

But remember the City is a conservative place, and there's only a short leash for personal eccentricity in clothes. Darren dresses the part and would wear anything with a designer label on the outside – notably his Italian designer suits (Armani, Versace) and items from Paul Smith and Browns – but he is careful to save the flamboyant items for social life.

A woman in a man's world

Charlotte is operating in a man's world and so her clothes have to sustain her credibility and can't be too outrageous. She always wears suits in dark colours – or at least jackets and skirts – and has just got used to the idea that she can afford Nicole Farhi and Jasper Conran even when it is not sale time. Skirts in the City will never be as short as they are in the West End, and the men are rather terrified of the idea of a power-dressing shoulder-padded woman. Charlotte normally shops in Knightsbridge and South Molton Street (she adores Browns), but still finds herself slipping into the City branch of Austin Reed when she's in a hurry.

The Ladies Who Lunch

The main clothes explosion is outside the City: wives of City men, who would have led blameless fashion-free lives ten years ago, now have a lot of money to spend. An English edition of the American magazine *W* has been launched just in order to tell these New Rich how to spend it and where to wear it. The Ladies Who Lunch are the mainstay of the current fashion boom: who else could afford £2,000 of Chanel each season? Over lunch in Wilton's they talk labels: YSL, Ferre, Yohji, Joseph, Ozbek, Blahnik, Frizon, Galliano. . . .

Trinkets and Toys

The Filofax is essential for Charlotte's busy social life. She bought one with an ostrich-skin cover for herself and another for an ex-boyfriend in eelskin. This caused quite a lot of trouble – unfortunately the eelskin wiped the magnetic codes off his credit cards, which left him looking pretty silly one night in the smart Chelsea restaurant Fifty-One, Fifty-One, with two clients and £200 worth of blackened redfish to pay for.

Love from Mont Blanc

Everything's done electronically nowadays of course, but sometimes the Slicker is motivated to write something down on paper – a postcard from Mont Blanc perhaps. For this, biros and Pentels are most definitely out. For years the only fountain pen to be seen with was the Montblanc Meisterstück 149, the big black brute which was perfect for signing contracts. Lately it has been challenged by other big black brutes from Parker, Pelikan, Waterman and Sheaffer, but at £160 the Montblanc remains the acme of plain plastic pens. Of course, you can spend thousands on diamond-encrusted Crosses and Lamys, but it's just not the same.

Waterproof to any depth

In the watchmanship stakes too one brand is pre-eminent. The gold Rolex is the basic entry-level dealer's watch. Like the Montblanc pen, it's made in two sizes to suit men and women. Without exception, the City women all use the men's sizes: the strap of Charlotte's Oyster Perpetual had to be specially shortened to stay on her delicate wrist. Darren's, waterproof to any depth he can sink to, was an unbirthday present to himself after he made £10,000 on the Sock Shop flotation. The rule with watches is that if it's not Swiss, it's not a watch – this is one place where you won't see a Citizen, Seiko, Sekonda or Timex. Omegas are just about acceptable; Audemars-Piguet, Baume & Mercier or Patek Philippe show an unhealthy interest in watchmaking as jewellery and make a completely different statement about you.

There is an ever-expanding market in portable equipment, including the Reuter Pocketwatch, and the portable phone is now an essential part of life. You can even have a small fax fitted to your car. But who wants to be wheeling and dealing 24 hours a day?

POSERS'
PLAYTHINGS

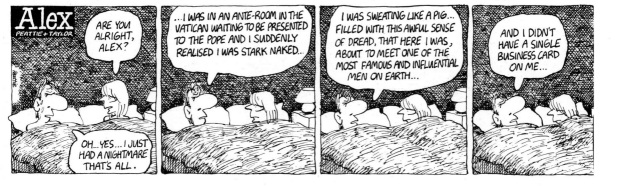

-11- *TIME OFF*

INSTANT SUNSHINE

Holidays are difficult for City people. Not for them reading a brochure in January and booking a package for August: Jesus Christ, who knows what'll be happening in August? If you're in Mergers and Acquisitions, and you've booked your holiday of a lifetime, £3,000 and three weeks in Tibet, and if your boss tells you at 30 minutes' notice to cancel and be on a plane to New York, you'd better be booked in at the Sherry Holland tomorrow or you won't have a job. They pay you well, but your private life is entirely at their disposal too. Although, to be fair, when you leave the firm you can repurchase your soul at reasonable terms on a lease-back basis.

British Virgins

Time off, therefore, is arranged at the last moment. Phuket in Thailand is the current favourite and, combined with a couple of nights at the Oriental in Bangkok, will really give you something to brag about on your return. The Mandarin in Hong Kong is the other top hotel, but the City Slicker prefers something more off-beat. The Maldives, Indonesia or a safari in Zimbabwe would be preferable to a holiday in Hong Kong. The Caribbean is as popular as ever, with the smaller islands, such as Grenada and Anguilla, becoming firm favourites, but if you actually want to get away from your phone the private resort islands in the Grenadines or British Virgins are the places for you.

Skiing is, of course, ideal for sudden expense-no-object trips, and you can even pop across for the weekend. Tahiti or Mexico with Club Med fit the bill in summer for the active Slicker. Like skiing, it is especially popular when there is a family to take. Everything may be included in the price, but at £700 a head per week the sums add up fast.

Darren managed three one-week escapes last year: one to Tunisia, one to St Kitts and one at Christmas to the Bahamas. Charlotte has a problem. Many of her friends, bright young things though they are, don't work in the City, and frankly can't afford Kenya or Mauritius or Mexico. So last year she slummed it with a couple of girlfriends in Lanzarote where – horrors! – she bumped into one of her firm's market-makers, lobster-red and loud-mouthed, in a hotel bar. Never again.

Pursuit to the death

The blue-blood, blue-chip grandees at the top of the City hierarchy have always

Peace at any price: Phuket in Thailand (take care how you pronounce it)

played hard at the traditional upper-class recreation of hunting, shooting and fishing. Now the amount of money available to City employees for conspicuous consumption has increased the numbers involved. And they don't just participate for pure pleasure: power and recreation has become the flip-side of the City-red-in-tooth-and-claw survival of the fittest in the financial markets.

Hunting has done well out of the upturn in the economy, and large numbers of City people have taken it up, often quite late in life. In its glamour, stylized violence, bad language and pursuit to the death, hunting has many parallels with everyday life in Mergers and Acquisitions. It is expensive, exhilarating and dangerous – 'the pleasures of war without the guilt'. It is also socially useful, and a surprising number of deals have been arranged at the stirrup-cup. In any hunt within 150 miles of London (except Surrey of course) you'll come across the unregulatable in pursuit of the uneatable. The Vodafone isn't yet part of the tackle, but it's coming.

Just OK riders usually spend their weekends in the Cotswold hunts; superior beings take days out with the Ferney, Belvoir and Pytchley. The costs are satisfyingly enormous: it'll cost at least £2,000 to buy your mount and around £4,000 annually to stable it, excluding the cost of transport, your immaculate and stylish clobber and the subscription to the hunt.

How to pot foreign clients

For a while, in the seventies, shooting seemed to be beyond the pocket of all but the richest Brit. But Slickers who can afford £700 a day, and the value to companies of entertaining foreign clients in a sport where they can rub shoulders with dukes (he voss chust like vun of uss!), have revitalized it. Even the shortage of game birds is being

acted upon – Merrill Lynch has recently given £30,000 to the Game Conservancy to help study grouse and their habitat.

Grouse is the top market bird, being wild (expensive), fast (up to 85 m.p.h.) and low-flying (bloody difficult to hit). They also taste reasonable. Grouse moors are, therefore, the ones with the highest social cachet. Savills, the estate agent which specializes in the buying and selling of grouse moors, say that the pressure to join the elite has pushed the price up 500% in the last ten years. They now cost up to £300 an acre, and start at around 2,500 acres. Recent purchasers include financier Christopher Moran, Sir Joseph Nickerson (despite being peppered by Viscount Whitelaw a few years ago), the Duke of Westminster and Sheikh Hamdam al Maktoum of Dubai. Property magnate Peter Jones and Jardine Matheson chairman Henry Keswick both have highly regarded grouse moors.

Almost all the top two hundred moors are syndicated or rented for part of the season, but they can scarcely be regarded as good investments. Savills reckon that the return on capital might be 1 or 2% if all the

THIS SPORTING LIFFE

Let a little hunting help you scent out that hostile bid

DON'T SHOOT THE HOST

It's freezing cold I hate Scotland I've never liked heather it's really annoying every time I go out for a fly some overweight merchant banker starts shooting at me...

GROUSE.

shooting was rented out. Jim Slater got his fingers badly burned trying to make a Scottish estate, Tulchan, a paying proposition. But nobody buys one to make money – or at least not directly. Many feel there is no better way to inform old money and new of the resources of the City than standing with its owners on a freezing Scottish hillside dressed in damp, scratchy tweed while attempting to hit an impossible target at £40 a go. Peppering easier targets such as beaters and one's host count as social gaffes.

£3,500 fishes

Fly-fishing for salmon is the last of the old-money triumvirate of sports, and it too has taken on a new aspect with new City wealth. Like grouse shooting, more and more people want to do it, just as the numbers of these tasty creatures are in decline. Prices have correspondingly become astronomical: to own a top-rank river costs around £3,500 for each fish caught per year. For example, the Conon near Inverness, on which 12 people can fish, was secretly sold by the Hydro-Board to Peter Whitfield for upwards of £1,500,000.

Whitfield is one of the leaders of the current fashionable trend in fishing, the time share. This allows Slickers to pay £30,000 for four weeks' fishing a year, two weeks in spring and two in autumn on two different rivers. It also allows the owner to recoup his capital outlay very rapidly.

Traditional upper-class pastimes have prospered in the bull market, but other less snooty occupations have also come into their own. For the young City rich there are lots of new sports – all they have to be is exciting and expensive, preferably involving large amounts of impressive-looking equipment and clothing.

Helicopter Skiing

Skiing naturally fits the bill. It has enjoyed an enormous rise in popularity, but nowhere more so than in the City. From Christmas onwards around half of non-business conversations are concerned with snow – where it is, how much there is and how to get there. Everyone rapidly becomes desensitized to all the piste/pissed jokes. There are few young brokers who don't take at least one week and more, probably two, on the slopes. Currently the French resorts colonized by Sloanes, like Val d'Isère, are most popular with the early twenties. They try the smarter and more expensive Swiss resorts like Klosters and Gstaad as they get older. Here, you will find insider dealer Gerard profitably mixing with the Eurobankers, even though his Vodafone doesn't work in Switzerland. Really serious ski-smarties go helicopter skiing in the Rockies; whole days on unspoilt off-piste powder, using the chopper as a sophisticated chairlift or, if necessary, a rapid transit ambulance.

Some securities firms like to encourage business by taking amenable fund managers away for 'winter conferences' – lo-o-ong weekends in fashionable resorts with an hour-long 'seminar' on investment opportunities in Nepal on the first morning as an excuse. However, the Crash of '87 put paid to the freebies, and it may be some time before firms feel they can be so lavish again.

Windsurfing has caught on a great deal, particularly with Darren and his mates – he first learnt on a Club 18-30 holiday in Lanzarote. A club has now opened up in the 'revitalized' Docklands. Where once the wealth of an empire was moved, wet-suited brokers skim across the still basins.

Yachting has some adherents, though it requires more time and dedication than most Slickers can spare. They like the short sharp shock of spontaneous fun: the now annual 'Merket' rally from London to Monte Carlo, run by the charming Anton Bilton, is more their sort of thing. Fast cars, giggly young women, champagne by the crate and irresponsibility all have considerable appeal to the Hooray Henrys fresh out of the Blues and Royals.

The 100 m.p.h. teatray

Many of these army types are members of the winter sports fraternity in Switzerland, and get their kicks by touching 100 m.p.h. on a teatray down the Cresta run. The lunatic fringe of this already seriously unstable group are in the Dangerous Sports Club. This society, which operates rather like a division of EXIT without the soul-searching, and whose surviving members are now in their early thirties, has recently registered under the Business Expansion Scheme in order to capitalize on the film

and TV rights of their activities. You know the sort of thing – bungee-jumping off the Clifton Suspension Bridge tethered with elastic ropes; dinner parties in the craters of active volcanos (Clive, this wine's sulphurized); putting a double-decker bus on skis and taking it down a black run.

Golf is the passion of the Japanese, for whom only the best will do. You can see them putting away at Wentworth, Rye or the Royal and Ancient. Private investor Peter plays off 11. Business takes him to Liverpool more often than it should: he conducts it on the course at Lytham.

The English Season

Forget about participation sports – what about spectator sports? Much of the gilded glamour of the supreme occasions of the English Season would be rather pinchbeck without the money and attention the City gives them. Royal Ascot, Wimbledon, Henley, the Derby – all do extremely well out of the desire of firms to entertain their clients (and more particularly their wives) with all the luxury and social *éclat* that only

ANOTHER SORT OF POWDER

Fast, competitive, dangerous ... just like life in the Square Mile

CASHING IN ON THE UPPER CRUST

English upper-class life can provide. Typical costs per person are as follows:

Men's final at Wimbledon	£555
Women's final at Wimbledon	£295
England v Wales at Twickenham	£245
British Grand Prix at Silverstone	£189

Without a doubt, *the* event is Wimbledon, and no one turns down an invitation. What better way to show your high-rolling clients how much you appreciate their business, and have a pretty bloody marvellous time yourself looking after them? D'Arcy thinks so, and his wife agrees.

At Wimbledon each year the most fortunate companies possess debenture seats for the Centre Court: a snip at £6,000 each, they are effectively five-year season tickets. Others have to apply six months in advance and hope to be lucky in the ballot, or scrabble among the touts. There are 44 tents in the grounds for 'entertainment facilities', i.e. very large amounts of smoked salmon, champagne, and strawberries and cream. One of the most galling experiences for the real tennis fan who manages, through great good fortune, to obtain a ticket for the Centre Court is to see all the empty seats whose occupants are too relaxed to leave the hospitality tent, where they occasionally glance at the match on television as they crack open another Pol Roger. The waiting list for tents is very long, and pressure from firms eager to spend the company's money on pleasure has caused the All-England Lawn Tennis and Croquet Club to ration facilities. Merrill Lynch used to have an on-site tent for two weeks, and now they are reduced to six days.

Striped blazer exhibitionists

But, though Wimbledon is far and away the biggest draw, and very suitable for foreigners in general and Americans in particular, it is jolly expensive and also very difficult to talk serious money at length when set and match points keep getting in the way just as the mark was metaphorically about to sign on the chalked line. Now this is not the sort of thing that happens at the Henley Royal Regatta. Probably less than 10% of the crowd pay any attention to what's happening on the water, and many are oblivious to any external stimuli at all, as Pimms and champagne wreak their revenge. Flirtations and striped blazer exhibitionism are the major occupations, and as long as you can keep your client reasonably lucid by gently rationing the fizz, you can talk shop all day. Of course, it's very English indeed, and it's not the sort of thing the Japanese are going to cancel appointments for, but it works very well with British

clients. On July evenings at Kensington and Chelsea pubs squiffy young brokers are seen in their boaters and blazers reliving the alcoholic triumphs of the day. They are easily spotted by their surrounding crowd of very pretty, very giggly young girls in summer dresses and big floppy hats. They usually end up at the 151 Club in the King's Road, where one of the girls will be sick.

Bartered boxes

Royal Ascot is another major hospitality event, but like Wimbledon the pressure for facilities is enormous. There are 280 boxes, each of which holds 12-14 people. Three-quarters of these are rented by companies, the rest by private individuals. Trying to obtain a box for your company is almost impossible – the waiting list has 560 names on it and the last box changed hands in 1969. When companies with boxes don't use them, they are meant to offer them for sub-letting through the racecourse organizers. They don't, of course. They do it privately and make around ten times as much – maybe £9,000 on Gold Cup day.

The world's most famous race, the Derby, is not as glamorous from a business point of view. The facilities are rather more spartan than at Ascot. Instead of boxes there are 198 viewing pens, which are merely cordoned-off areas of grass. Each holds eight people and costs £1,500 a season. Turnover is brisker than for the Ascot boxes, but still only around 5% come up each year. Epsom intends building a new grandstand with proper boxes before 1991, so the Derby may begin to rival Ascot.

Owning a racehorse has always been a badge of extreme wealth and conspicuous consumption – it puts you up there with Robert Sangster and the Royal Family; but, even for the City, it requires severe amounts of the folding stuff, and unless you are

particularly lucky, you'll probably never see any of it again. A potential Classic horse will normally cost anything between 50,000 guineas and several million dollars. To keep it in training will cost at least £15,000 annually, plus insurance, vets' bills, travelling expenses and entry fees (several thousand pounds a time for Group 1 races). Of the 14,000 horses in training in the UK, more than half will never win any prize money. Of all foals born in the UK only a third will be racing as two-year-olds.

However, it is possible to make a 100% return on capital within two years if your horse wins a serious race (Jeff Smith, chief executive of the AIM Group, bought Chief Singer for 10,000 guineas in 1982; by August 1984 he had come second in the 2,000 Guineas, and won the St James's Palace Stakes, the July Cup and the Swettenham Stud Sussex Stakes. His – tax-free – winnings came to £200,000 and his value at stud was around £5 million). This is the sort of gamble which appeals to the new City: the involvement of large sums, make or break, jackpot or wipe-out, making a killing

UP THERE WITH THE ROYALS

Hedging your bets with hospitality: corporate entertainers like showing off at Ascot

SLOANES GO TO THE DOGS

through specialist knowledge (or inside information), and – perhaps, most of all – the whole thing is over in a couple of adrenalin-filled minutes.

More and more horses are now run in partnerships (up to four owners) or syndicates (up to 12) which reduces costs to a reasonable couple of thou a year and still allows a broker to take impressionable young women to the races to watch 'his' horse. But recently a curious social eddy has brought many Sloane brokers and bankers to participation in a less aristocratic form of racing. They spend their evenings at London's dog-racing tracks, more usually considered the natural habitat of Arthur Daley lookalikes in car-coats. They have discovered the simple pleasures of a night at the dogs: a surprisingly good meal with a large amount to drink, intermittently enlivened by watching your money run after mechanical vermin. The pleasures of this sport have encouraged many of them (women as well as men) to take a share in Lightning Lads and Deptford Flashes.

Mobile Sumo wrestlers at Twickers

The Essex Boys are Hammers supporters to a man, but as West Ham haven't trodden the Wembley turf since 1980 they haven't had a lot to crow about. Soccer is not a City sport; the image is completely wrong. Cricket is totally incomprehensible to all foreigners, as indeed it is to most Brits, so anyone with tickets to Lords usually goes with an old cricketing pal rather than a colleague or prospect. Rugby is quite different, and Charles is to be found in the West Car Park at Twickenham twice a year. Champagne or Ruddles beer is the tipple, certainly not light and bitter. This is all very agreeable to his Japanese guests, who seem to be partial to rugby as it presumably reminds them of mobile Sumo wrestlers. Twickenham's car parks have hospitality tents where crowds of Welsh businessmen, lighter by £250 for a champagne lunch and a match ticket, tend to riot if their tickets fail to materialize.

Opera has always had strong links with the City. Sir Claus Moser, a director of Rothschild's, has just left after 13 years as unpaid chairman of the Royal Opera House. Jeremy Isaacs of Channel 4 Television has replaced him, but both Robin Leigh-Pemberton, the Governor of the Bank of England, and Jacob Rothschild were strong contenders. Robin Hambro is the organizing director of the Royal Opera House Trust, and there can scarcely be a firm of bankers or brokers that doesn't have a regular box. Opera uniquely combines cultural excellence with the highest social prestige. What could be more gratifying for a firm's image than sponsoring a production, as bullion dealers Mocatta & Goldsmid did for *Der Rosenkavalier*, and filling the first-night house with one's favoured contacts from the Cabinet, the Treasury and the Bank of England downwards?

Angels with hearts of gold

Glyndebourne too has the bankers' support; without an Arts Council subsidy it enthusiastically seeks business sponsorship. These 'angels' have included Citicorp, Dresdener Bank, Deutsche Bank, NatWest, Barclays and the Midland. The price of this image building starts at around £100,000. And there's no need to all rush out at once to sponsor a production: they're booked up until 1991. The majority of the audience is thus composed largely of businessmen, and those without City contacts find it hard to get tickets, except those advertised in *The Times* classified ads at a considerable mark-up. Even the Friends of Glyndebourne have a ballot for tickets. Glyndebourne also has the reputation of the toughest poker-school among chauffeurs in the south-east. Real show-offs take helicopters from London.

The theatre has never had any particular link with the City but in 1987 Caryl Churchill's satirical play, *Serious Money*, opened at the Royal Court Theatre. A scarifying attack on the City, it received excellent reviews and did such good business during its run that it transferred to the West End. A little-remarked aspect of its success, however, is that large numbers of its appreciative audience are the objects of its barbed wit. Even at the radical Royal Court in Sloane Square, BMWs and Porsches were double-parking round the corner to attend the show.

ARIAS OF MUTUAL INTEREST

Power-picnicking at Glyndebourne

GLOSSARY

Words in italic appear as a separate entry

ACCOUNT
Stock Exchange term for the period, usually two weeks, sometimes three, during which shares are traded. The Account Day is the last day of each account and Settlement Day, the Monday ten days later, is the day when settlement has to be made.

ACCOUNT TRADING
Buying and selling within the account so that the cash for the transaction does not have to be found, only what you lose – if you lose. If you win you get a cheque on Settlement Day. A further advantage of account trading is that only one set of commission is charged by the broker. A disadvantage is the temptation to trade beyond your means.

ADRs
American Depository Receipts. As US citizens cannot buy foreign shares direct, ADRs are certificates issued by a bank showing that a specific number of a company's shares have been deposited with it. They are priced in US dollars and then traded like any other American security.

ALPHA BETA GAMMA DELTA
These are classifications of shares post-Big Bang. The largest and most marketable shares, about 60, are Alphas, the next 500 Betas, and the rest, provided there are at least two market-makers prepared to make prices in them, are Gammas. Deltas are those where trades need to be matched, i.e. you must find a seller for a buyer, and vice versa. Dealing rules vary. For Alphas and Betas the market-makers must deal at the prices they are showing on the screen. For Gammas and Deltas the prices are just an indication. That's the theory, anyway. When it really matters, when things are on the move, the rules get bent a little.

ARBITRAGEUR
Strictly speaking a buyer and ultimately a seller of shares in a takeover situation in an overseas country, it has now come to mean anyone who buys a significant and therefore influential stake in any company involved in a takeover. By buying shares in a company where a bid has been made, the arbitrageur is supposed to be taking the risk that the takeover may be fought off and the shares will fall back. This has happened on several occasions recently, e.g. BTR failing to get Pilkington, Dixons to get Woolworths, Blue Circle to get Birmid. But in the heady days of 1985 and 1986, the arbs usually made a killing because each takeover produced two or three successively higher bids. King of the Arbs was, of course, Ivan Boesky – but then with his knowledge he would be, wouldn't he?

ASSET STRIPPER
Someone who buys a company and sells off some of its assets, hopefully for as much as or more than he paid for the whole company. He is then left with a company which is still trading plus a pile of cash, the stripper most probably having made the bid with shares in the first place. The practice acquired a bad name in the Slater Walker era of the early seventies, thanks to the brash activities of some former employees of Slater Walker. John Bentley and Christopher Selmes spring readily to mind.

AT-THE-MONEY
A *put or call option* whose *exercise price* is approximately the same as the current price of the underlying security (see *in-the-money option* and *out-of-the money option*).

AVERAGING
Buying a share again, usually at a lower price than your first purchase, to get a better 'average' price.

BALLOT
When a *new issue* is oversubscribed, some or all of the applications are put into a hat and drawn at random so that all or part of the original application is granted.

BEAR
A pessimist who sells in anticipation of falling prices.

BEAR HUG
A notice to a company's board that a *Tender Offer* is imminent or under consideration. A Teddy Bear Hug is when the target company expresses satisfaction with the merger but only at a higher price.

BEAR MARKET
Going down. Or, as Darren would say to a reluctant seller, 'It's going DAHN! Look I'll spell it for you: Dee Oh Double-you Enn.'

BED AND BREAKFAST
If your broker bumbles on to you about bed and breakfast he is doing the standard early spring *churning* ploy of getting you to sell and buy back to establish capital losses, or possibly, though for more obscure reasons, capital gains, before the end of the tax year. It means selling a stock one evening – the bed bit – and buying it back the next morning – the breakfast bit. If you had bought Blue Arrow at 168p in September 1987, and in March 1988 you realized you were faced with a capital gains tax bill on all those lovely gains you made in early 1987, and you were also convinced that Blue Arrow was a good long-term hold, then you might sell at 109 one evening and buy back at 114 the next morning, establishing your loss from 168 to 109.

Before you do it, make sure that you really are faced with a hefty capital gains tax liability. And work out the sums. It hurts a bit to sell at 109 and immediately buy back at 114 (these spreads have certainly widened since the Crash), even if you do only pay one set of commission because it is within the *account*. Remember, too, that the Inland Revenue have disallowed a claim where they proved the sale was purely for tax purposes.

BLOW HIS TITS OFF
Expression used by money brokers meaning 'Sell it to him now'.

BLUE BUTTON
A trainee *stockbroker* allowed to collect prices but not to transact dealings.

BLUE CHIPS
The very largest companies quoted on the Stock Exchange. The term derives from the colour of the most expensive chips in a poker game. There is no specific number of blue chip companies nor even any qualifying criterion. The term is used, for example, to describe companies that are in the FT30 Index. Tel, our market-maker, would know

them as *Alpha* stocks and would have them on his screens in Ls. Thus they are very marketable and unlikely to go bust.

BULL
An optimist who buys a stock or share in the expectation that its price will rise.

BULL MARKET
Going up.

BUSINESS EXPANSION SCHEME
A scheme introduced in the early 1980s to encourage the better-paid, by way of tax relief, to invest in new companies. Tax relief can be claimed provided the investor keeps his investment in the qualifying company for five years. It has been subject to constant revision in each Budget since its introduction. There are limits on both the amount that can be raised under the scheme and the amount of tax relief available to any single investor.

BUTTERFLY
When you find a Butterfly, put the Bollinger in the fridge. It's a no-lose situation in traded options where the prices in a stock are such that you can write two positions and buy one in between. Whichever way the price moves, you win. Like the Orinoco Purple Emperor, the Butterfly is very rare, and you have to move very fast indeed to catch it.

BUY INS
Buy ins were made legal by the Companies Act of 1981, and since then several respectable companies such as GEC, J. Rothschild Holdings and Mountleigh have bought their own shares. If the shares are trading below asset value it makes good sense – Mountleigh's were – or if you want to improve your EPS (earnings per share) it is a simple way of doing it. It can be abused, and there are safeguards like shareholder approval at an AGM or EGM.

BUYING ON MARGIN
All investors need to understand this term, because if they ever get tempted to do it they should know the risks they are running. In simple terms it means buying stocks or *futures*, only putting up a fraction of the money and borrowing the rest, probably at fairly punitive rates

of interest. It is wonderful when things are going up. Who cares if you have to pay 15 per cent interest on £100,000 when the stocks will soon be worth £150,000? You love it, the bank loves it, your broker loves it. When the turn comes and the £100,000 worth of stock is worth £70,000, you are faced with two alternatives – provide more security for the bank because the collateral has suddenly dropped by £30,000, or sell and find the £30,000 plus costs yourself. If many of the stocks were high-fliers that are now suddenly unsaleable, you are in Beeg Trouble. This simple example shows you why the goodies like ICI and Glaxo come crashing down even more than the baddies like Rotaprint. You must sell; you can't sell Rotaprint; so you have to sell ICI.

Buying on margin became one of the scapegoats of the Wall Street Crash of 1929, and the Americans thought they had made a recurrence impossible by not allowing stock purchases unless 50 per cent of the price was paid. The punters found a way round that. They dabbled and then fell in love with first the futures market and then the *options* market. Back we go to speculation, with only 10 per cent of the money up-front. Being inventive and competitive, the Americans then developed a real gambler's financial instrument – options on futures.

CABINET
Basically bad news. It means the value has sunk to nothing. If your broker tells you the price of your traded option is Cabinet to 2, it means it will cost you 2 (or 1,000 × 2 in fact) to buy any more, but on the other hand you will get nothing if you want to sell the *option* you bought with such confidence two weeks ago.

CALL OPTION
See *put* and *call options*.

CAPS AND COLLARS
Arrangements to borrow money at variable rates of interest but with a guarantee that the rate will not rise above or move below certain levels.

CHARTISTS
People who predict what will happen to a share price, based on what has happened in the past, by means of various

devices such as line charts, bar charts, pie charts and point and figure diagrams. They love playing with Apple Mac computers. It is a little-known fact that nobody has ever come away better informed from looking at a pie chart.

CHINESE WALLS
Invisible barriers in internal communication between different areas of the new financial conglomerates – the left hand tries hard not to let the right hand know what it is doing. They are necessary because one arm of a conglomerate may be selling a company's shares while another arm is plotting the same company's takeover. There's a certain conflict of interest here, and when times get tough and profits get scarce the effectiveness of Chinese Walls will be severely tested.

CHURNING
Describes a practice which has been the subject of much criticism. Where a broker or fund manager has control of discretionary funds he can generate income for himself by churning: buying and selling stocks or switching from Shell to BP just for the sake of generating commission. Clearly the temptation increases when markets go quiet, volumes are low and the overheads are high.

COMFORT DEAL
Effectively a guarantee that if you buy some shares the person giving you the comfort will buy them from you, or arrange for someone else to buy them from you, at a price at least equal to what you paid. It would almost certainly be illegal if the company offering the deal was using its own money to buy its own shares.

COMPLIANCE
Self policing by financial institutions, nearly all of whom now have a Compliance Officer.

CONCERT PARTY
An arrangement whereby two or more parties agree to buy or sell a company's shares, either to move the price or take a significant holding. It was made illegal in this country after the plethora of takeovers in the late sixties and seventies, when Jim Slater and his cronies would take major stakes in targets in

conjunction with others – i.e. others in the concert party. Other stock market operators have been accused of it – for example David Wickins and Michael Ashcroft in the takeover of Henlys, but they were cleared.

CORPORATE RAIDER
An individual or company who buys a significant stake in another company with a view to making a quick profit on the stake or as a prelude to a full takeover bid.

CROWN JEWELS
As you might expect, these are a company's most valuable assets. They are not always apparent even to the owners of the company itself: for example the Country Gentlemen's Association did not appreciate the value of their mailing list. But usually they are only too apparent and can be sold or optioned off to make the company less attractive to a bidder. When Hanson was bidding for SCM in America, SCM came to an agreement with Merrill Lynch that they would buy two of its most valuable assets if an outsider acquired more than a third of its equity. Hanson fought this deal in the courts and won.

DAISY CHAIN
Nasty practice whereby market manipulators give the appearance of activity in shares so as to lure in genuine investors.

DAWN RAID
If you are the subject of a dawn raid it will mean that a raider has bought a substantial number of your shares from one or several institutions before anyone is aware of what is happening. Dawn raids were common in the early eighties but are less so now, for two reasons. First, it was considered unfair to the majority of shareholders if one or two substantial holders were offered a special deal. Secondly, the converse was true: the special deal often turned out to be a bum deal, as the raid was usually the prelude to a bid which would often be forced up, and the institutions who sold in the dawn raid were made to look silly. Dawn raids surfaced again immediately after the Crash of '87, when institutional liquidity was low and cash was king. The mood had passed even by December when a dawn raid on Blue

Circle, supposedly by Hanson, failed miserably.

DEAD CAT BOUNCE
If you drop a cat from the top of the NatWest Tower, it will bounce first before falling back to the ground. It will then almost certainly be dead. Similarly if market prices drop sharply from a great height they bounce up, largely because people who sold *short* have to buy back to complete the transaction. Like the moggie, the market then falls again. We had a great Dead Cat Bounce in October 1987. Down sharply on Monday, down sharply on Tuesday, bounce on Wednesday, down again for the next two weeks. This situation is also known, less evocatively, as a Spike.

DEATH VALLEY CURVE
Describes all kinds of risky speculations, but most usually means the touch-and-go period when a start-up company has used up all its equity capital to fund the start-up before the cash-flow has become positive. The crucial decision is: do we stay with it or do we let it fall off into Death Valley?

DOG
A company or share that has performed badly for years and seems to have poor prospects as in 'God, what a dog of a share that is.'

DOW JONES
The Dow Jones Industrial Average Index. Similar to the FT30, it consists of the average of 30 blue chip companies on the New York Stock Exchange and provides a general indicator of the movement of prices.

DROP DEAD FEE
A fee paid by a bidder to a lender who has made a line of credit available for a bid that has failed. It means that a bidder can commit himself to big money without having to take it if it fails. The term probably originated when a miffed bidder, when asked whether he still wanted the money, told the banker to drop dead.

DROP LOCK
A floating rate bond that automatically switches to fixed-rate interest if rates fall below a predetermined point.

EQUITIES
General term for ordinary shares in companies.

EUROBOND
International bonds issued outside the domestic market of the issuer by a syndicate of international banks.

EX DIVIDEND
Dividends are paid regularly to shareholders, usually twice a year, and in order to facilitate administration there is a certain day, usually the first of a Stock Exchange *account*, when a company is quoted ex (without) dividend.

EXECUTION ONLY
The operation by a broker in carrying out purchases or sales of securities, without research or other advisory services, with consequent reduction in commission charge.

EXERCISE PRICE
The price at which the buyer or seller of an *option* may buy or sell the underlying security.

FAN CLUB
Legal, as opposed to the *Concert Party*, which isn't. Several people independently and coincidentally decide to buy shares in a certain company. The heavy buying of Guinness shares at the end of the bid for Distillers was done by either a Concert Party or a Fan Club. The trials will tell us which.

FLOTATION
The issuing of shares to the public in a new company on the stock market.

FOOTSIE
FTSE – the Financial Times Stock Exchange 100 Share Index, which was established in 1982 to give a broader and more representative feel of the market than the FT30 Index, which had been the main market barometer since 1935. The Footsie is a moving measurement of the share prices of 100 leading companies on the Stock Exchange, calculated every minute.

FRONT RUNNING
In the old days a broker got the best price for his client and, if the *jobber* happened to have a lot of stock and could sense a determined buyer, he could mark his price up and good luck to

him. But now, with the integrated conglomerates, what happens if the market-making arm builds a big position in a stock because it knows the analyst in the conglomerate is going to recommend that stock? We cannot be sure what happens, but the practice is called front running. In early 1987 an exceptionally ethical motors analyst at Phillips & Drew loudly protested about the firm's demands that he make his recommendations known to the firm's market-makers, and left for the broker James Capel which does not make markets and can therefore be perceived as giving impartial advice. Capel's competitors say that while it does not make a price for others it certainly acts as a heavy trader itself, so could still do a bit of front running.

FUTURES
Contracts for the delivery or purchase of assets at a future date.

GEARING UP
The practice of borrowing money to increase a holding.

GILTS
British government securities. Originally the certificates had gilded edges – hence 'gilts'. No British government has ever failed to meet its capital or interest obligations on such securities.

GOLDEN SHARE
A share retained, usually but not necessarily by the government, giving the holder ultimate control of a company, sometimes indefinitely and sometimes for a limited and specified period of time.

GOING PUBLIC
See *flotation*.

GOLDEN HANDCUFFS
In short, a financial inducement to retain a key executive. In the early days of the run-up to Big Bang it was thought that a significantly higher salary would be sufficient. Subsequently it became necessary to add hefty bonuses which would only be paid at the end of an executive's contract.

GOLDEN PARACHUTE AND SILVER WHEELCHAIR
These terms are synonymous and refer to employment contract provisions very often put in place to prevent a takeover or at least make it a bloody sight more expensive. If the bidder is still not deterred, he will find the directors jumping out and floating gently to the ground underneath their golden parachutes or being pushed off home in their silver wheelchairs.

GREENMAIL
A chunk of money paid to get rid of a *corporate raider* for his block of shares that he has bought, threatening a takeover. It had its day in the USA – hence green for greenbacks – but as the price paid is at a premium it runs into all sorts of rules and regulations in Britain. Sir James Goldsmith received a great deal of greenmail in the early eighties. It made a welcome change from a little hate mail he received in the late seventies.

GREY MARKET
Nothing did more to make brokers realize that many of Thatcher's army of new investors did not understand the stock market, or if they did it was not the one where My Word Is My Bond. In the privatization issues some brokers established a grey market before shares were issued and before dealings started officially. In one or two of the issues – British Telecom, for example – when dealings officially started, the price was soon considerably higher. Yes, you've guessed it: some of those who had sold in the grey market refused to deliver the stock and sold it at a higher price in the real market. The brokers found themselves 'Dk'd', i.e. the punter said he 'Didn't Know' of the transaction.

HAMMERED
A *stockbroker* who cannot meet his obligations is hammered. The term stems from the custom of a Stock Exchange official called a waiter, who used to strike the arm of his seat three times to bring the floor to silence.

HAWAII
Expression used by money brokers, meaning 50 million.

HEAD AND SHOULDERS
The movement of a share price which, when written out in chart form, looks like a head and shoulders. The *chartist* would then tell you where the share price is going – down to the waist or up through the hat.

IDB
Inter-dealer brokers are becoming increasingly important for placing stock between market-makers.

IG INDEX
There are two bookies in the financial markets – City Index, which also does some sporting bets, and the IG Index. Betting on the Index is easy – you place your stake and decide which way the market will move. Get it right and your stake is multiplied by the number of points it moves. Get it wrong and you lose not only your stake, as in horse-racing, but also your stake multiplied by the number of points. You could have had a great week with £1,000 in October 1987. Lose £250,000, lose another £250,000, win £100,000, and so on.

As with all such operations there is the famous – or is it notorious – *Spread*. Spreads, as you will already have discovered, do not work in your favour. So don't think that because the *Footsie* is at 1800 you can put on £100 and if it rises to 1810 you've made £1,000. By the time you've coped with both the spread when you buy at 1800, and the one when you sell at 1810, you would barely be breaking even.

It's not like shares – you're not buying anything. It's not like *options* or *futures* – you're not buying the right to anything. You're just gambling on the price changing. Most people, apparently, are bullish and more than half lose money – in some cases big money. In the Crash several lost £500,000 and many lost £150,000. Bad debts are a problem. City Index expected to have £3 million of them in 1987.

IN-THE-MONEY OPTION
A *call option* whose *exercise price* is below the current market price of the underlying security.

JOBBER
Before Big Bang, jobbers were the dealers on the Stock Exchange floor through whom the *stockbrokers* had to buy and sell shares. They had no direct contact with the public. They are now called market-makers.

JUNK BONDS
Just what they sound like. Loans that are risky, most probably not secured and therefore carrying a higher rate of interest. It is a term and a practice common in the USA but will become more frequent here. Alec Monk implied that John Fletcher's loans for taking over his Dee Corporation were pretty junky. The tactic worked. Fletcher failed.

KERB TRADING
As well as in Shepherd's Market at night kerb trading takes place in the City by day, especially at the London Metal Exchange. It stems from trading done outside the two official five-minute 'rings'. It can also apply to telephone dealing after market hours. You will hear commentators refer to 'the late kerb'.

LADY MACBETH GAMBIT
See *White Knight*.

LEVERAGED BID
A bid for a company where the predator is borrowing money to make the bid.

LOCK-UP
An agreement between a target and a bidder to discourage other bidders. The lock-up could include an option to buy the *Crown Jewels*. It should really be called a close-out.

MULTIPLE APPLICATION
Prior to the BT flotation it was common practice for *stags* to make many small applications for a *new issue* as opposed to one large application, to increase chances of getting shares. To the surprise of many, most notably MP Keith Best, the practice suddenly became frowned upon.

NAKED POSITION
Not the Lloyd's secretary in the sixties who apparently enjoyed a three o'clock bonk with her underwriting boss in his 'box' every day. It is an unhedged position in the *futures* and *options* market and can leave you feeling very naked, as the trainee accountant discovered on 19 October 1987 when he went naked to the tune of £1 million.

NEW ISSUES
Shares being traded on the stock market for the first time.

NEW TIME
Purchase or sale of shares in one *account*, which are to be settled after the following account. Such a transaction is possible in the last two days of the account. Beware - a slightly different price could be quoted.

NIKKEI DOW
The Japanese equivalent of the FT Index and *Dow Jones Index*.

OPEN OUTCRY
Most trading in *futures* happens by word of mouth in the trading pit. The traders shout and signal at each other; meanwhile the prices are recorded and displayed electronically.

OPTIONS
Non-returnable deposits that give you the right to buy or sell a share or currency at an agreed price some time in the future. However, the vast majority of traded option contracts are traded again rather than taken up. See *put and call options*.

OUT-OF-THE-MONEY OPTION
A *call option* whose *exercise price* is above the current price of the underlying security.

PA
Personal account, an expression used by a fund manager or *stockbroker* to signify that he is buying or selling a share for himself and not for a client. It has been open to abuse in that a fund manager or stockbroker handling clients' money on a discretionary basis could buy a share and, if it went up during the *account* before settlement was due, keep it for himself, but if it went down he could unload it on his client. Theoretically, dealing for PA is now more difficult because in all conglomerates dealings have to be declared. Dealing PA for the account is definitely frowned on, even forbidden. But there are always friends...

PAPER
In City and investment terms paper is most important. Indeed many businessmen have made fortunes by using their 'paper' effectively. It means the shares which every company has but which when a company goes public become an easily tradable commodity. Thus if you are a private company and you want to buy another company for £10 million you will most probably have to find that £10 million in hard cash, because the vendors won't accept shares in a private company as they are virtually not negotiable. However, if you are a public company they will accept shares, your 'paper', because they know they can sell them (except in times of crisis like 1974 or October 1987).

PE RATIOS
Price/earnings ratios - Pee-ees - are calculated by dividing the company's share price by the earnings per ordinary share. PE ratios become increasingly important in *bull markets* as they signify how the market rates a share.

Investors buying shares for income (a *bear market* strategy) look at the yield, but those looking for capital growth (a bull market strategy) look at the PE ratio. If a share's PE ratio is higher than the market average the market is looking for above-average growth. What are considered growth companies can command PE ratios in the forties and fifties and even higher. These are high-risk, high-reward stocks. If they falter - and that can mean just a slowing down in the rate of growth - the market re-rates them instantly and bang! down they come 25, 50 or even 75%. It is very important to understand PEs.

PENNY SHARES
A colloquial term for very low-priced shares.

POISON PILL
Arrangement entered into by a target company, fearing a bid, to make itself less valuable to the bidder.

PORCUPINE PROVISION
See *Shark Repellent*.

PROGRAM TRADING
The automatic buying and selling of shares, *options* or *futures* according to computer-based programs.

PUT AND CALL OPTIONS
A put option is a contract which allows you to sell a fixed number of shares at a fixed price before a fixed time. A call option is a similar contract enabling you to buy shares in this way.

RAMP
It is possible for a group of investors to ramp a share either up or down by acting together and effectively creating a false market by giving the rest of the punters the impression that there are either more sellers or more buyers around than there really are.

REVERSE TAKEOVER
To obtain a public listing a private company can buy an existing publicly quoted company, often larger than itself. It can be a simpler method of obtaining a public quote than by the full preparation of an offering through the Stock Exchange.

ROLLOVER RELIEF
A method of carrying forward capital gains tax liabilities. It is relevant in cases where investors receive new shares by way of an exchange in a company takeover or where businesses sell a property asset that is shortly replaced with an alternative. Not to be confused with some Eurobond dealers' habits in the Great Eastern Hotel bedrooms on a quiet afternoon.

RUNNING THE BOOKS
The organization of a *new issue* of *securities* by a bank, keeping both borrower and underwriters informed.

RUNNING LONG AND SHORT
For a market-maker, running long means buying stock in most of the shares in which he makes a market. Running short means selling stock he does not own, anticipating a fall which will enable him to buy the stock at a lower price.

SAMURAI BOND
A Japanese term for a bond issued by a foreign entity in Japan, denominated in yen and purchased by non-residents of Japan.

SANDBAG
A stalling tactic used by a target company in the hope that either a *White Knight* or the US Cavalry will appear on the horizon.

SCALP
What Ricky does at FOX because of his limited capital – he trades for small gains, establishing and liquidating his positions continually in a short time.

SEAGULL
Term beloved of merchant bankers who circle over a client's head and then drop a strategy on his head.

SEAQ
Stock Exchange Automated Quotations system. The automated system which provides the prices at which transactions are made in the UK market under the new dual-capacity system. The prices are made available to brokers through *TOPIC*.

SECURITIES
Usually shares, debentures, government securities or *unit trusts* but also, strictly speaking, rights to money lent or deposited with an industrial and provident society or building society, but not any type of insurance policy.

SHARK REPELLENT
The use of corporate byelaws to prevent a hostile takeover. A *Porcupine Provision* is the same thing.

SHELL
A small and often non-trading company, usually with a public quote. Beloved of impatient entrepreneurs who reverse (see *reverse takeover*) their businesses into the shell to gain a public quotation, which allows them to grow faster by funding acquisitions using their *paper* as opposed to hard cash or cash hardly borrowed from the bank.

SHIP IT IN SHAG
Expression used by money brokers, meaning 'Buy it'.

SHOGUN BOND
Same as a *Samurai Bond* but in currencies other than yen.

SHORT OR SHORT SELLING
See *running long and short*.

SILVER WHEELCHAIR
See *Golden Parachute*.

SLEEPING POINT
If your investments keep you awake at night, sell down to the sleeping point.

SPIKE
See *Dead Cat Bounce*.

SPONSOR
The issuing house responsible for everything to do with a *new issue*.

SPREADS
The difference between the bid price – what the market-maker will pay you for shares – and the offer price – what he will sell them to you at, i.e. his profit.

STAG
Someone who buys a new issue and then sells it quickly for a short-term profit.

STOCKBROKER
Before Big Bang, the intermediary between the public and the *jobber*. He still exists, but within stockbroking firms there are now market-makers who can perform the functions of both broker and jobber.

STOP LOSS ORDER
An order placed to close a position automatically when a certain price is reached.

STRADDLE
A straddle is a technique of selling in one market, while simultaneously purchasing in another, the same *futures* contract.

STREAKER
A zero coupon bond, i.e. one with no interest, issued at a deep discount to give, by the time of redemption, a computed interest rate at face value on maturity.

SUCKERS' RALLY
Similar to the *Dead Cat Bounce* but over a longer timescale. On Wall Street in autumn 1929 the market fell a long way, but then in the spring of 1930 it recovered half the fall. This was a suckers' rally – anyone who bought then suffered two years of sliding prices. That was why in the spring of 1988 everyone was wary of buying.

SUSPENSION
The halting of trading in a share pending a major announcement – sometimes good (perhaps a takeover), sometimes bad (perhaps receivership).

TAKEOVER PANEL
Generally respected City body to oversee takeover bids, staffed by market practitioners on secondment. The respect it earned started well in the late sixties under Lord 'Nuremberg' Shawcross, but it then entered a long *bear market*, bottoming out in the mid eighties before rallying strongly when

Robert Alexander QC was appointed chairman in 1987.

TENDER OFFER

A public offer to buy some or all of the stock of a corporation within a specified period. The price offered is usually well above the current price of the shares to induce shareholders to offer their shares to the bidder.

THIRD MARKET

Literally that – the third market after the main and *USM* markets which trades Delta stocks, often in matched bargains. It comes under the auspices of the Stock Exchange, so it's quite legitimate, but it suffers from liquidity problems, i.e. it is difficult to buy and sell shares in sizeable quantities.

TOPIC

Teletext Output Price Information Computer. The communication system providing brokers with share price information as deals are struck.

TRIPLE WITCHING HOUR

The moment on the third Friday of March, June, September and December when *options* and *futures* contracts expire. They used to be called Quarter Days, and Lady Day, 25 March, was the most important because it was the last before the new fiscal year. It can pass off peaceably, or it can cause pandemonium and wild gyrations in prices.

UNDERWRITING

Issuing houses underwrite *new issues* to guarantee that they are fully taken up even if not fully subscribed by existing shareholders or the public.

UNIT TRUST

A trust formed to manage *securities* on behalf of a number of small investors.

USM

Unlisted Securities Market. The USM was introduced in 1980 as a subsidiary market to the main stock market to enable companies to raise extra capital without having to show the profit track record required for a full listing. After a slow start it has been a great success.

VENTURE CAPITAL

Risk capital offered by individuals or institutions to help fund new or developing businesses where the capital is provided in exchange for shares or equity rather than as a loan.

WHITE KNIGHT

A bidder who arrives to bid for a company and is welcomed by the company after it has received an offer from a Black Knight, who was unwelcome. A Grey Knight is a bidder who is welcome to neither the company nor the counter bidder. Guinness managed to be all three in its bid for Distillers. The Lady Macbeth Gambit comes in here somewhere. This is where the White Knight does the dirty and joins the Black Knight.

ACKNOWLEDGEMENTS

Alex cartoons reproduced from *The Independent* by kind permission of Peattie & Taylor

Original photography by Brian Harris of *The Independent*: 4, 5, 17-19, 22, 24, 34, 36, 39, 40, 45-6, 48-50, 62, 66-7, 70, 87, 110-1, 113-20, 122-3, 126-7

Newspaper cuttings from the John Frost Newspaper Service: 19, 77

Genesis Productions wish to thank the following for permission to reproduce photographs:

Associated Press Ltd: 65, 103, 104 below

BBC Hulton Picture Library: 8, 14

Elders IXL: 75

Financial Times: 12, 28, 47, 61, 64, 72, 76, 78, 82

Independent: Paul Grover 85; Brian Harris 7, 16, 98, 106-7, 133; Herbie Knott 100, 101 top; Jeremy Nicholl 131; David Rose 69, 83-4; David Sillitoe 33; Unknown 26; John Voos 137

Irving David: 96

Photo News Service: 95, 97

Popperfoto: 31-2, 42, 79, 94, 99, 101 above, 102, 104 right

Press Association: 10, 52, 68

Rex Features Ltd: 135

Thai Tourist Office: 130